Marriage According to His Book

God's Marriage Plan

Charlie P. Johnston Jr.

Marriage According to His Book

God's Marriage Plan

Marriage According to His Book
God's Marriage Plan

The Scriptures used throughout this book are quoted from the Authorized or King James Version unless otherwise noted. All explanatory insertions within a Scripture verse are enclosed in square brackets. All non-English words are printed with English letters and italicized.

Published by: **Johnston Publications**

3667 Northside Church Road
Greenwood, FL 32443

(850) 592-8769
www.johnstonpublications.com

ISBN: 0980176050
ISBN 13: 09780980176056
Library of Congress Catalogue Card Number: 2013916682
Published 2013
Printed in the United States of America

Dedication

To my beloved wife, Carol Ann Johnston; without her help this book might have gone unpublished. Also to our brothers and sisters born again of God's spirit, who are looking forward with anticipation to the blessed hope and return of Jesus Christ, our Living Lord and Savior. What a day that will be!

TABLE OF CONTENTS

PREFACE

❧

t has been a joyous adventure to study the depth of God's
Word pertaining to marriage. This book is offered with
a deep sense of humility. There is no claim on my part
to being a renowned marriage authority. However, God is
the expert on marriage. He alone has the first and the last
word about the subject of marriage because it's His institution. Today, nearly one out of two marriages end in divorce.
Clearly there is a vast gap of understanding among the general public about what marriage is, and is not. This book
is offered as a help and a guide to bring stability, strength,
and stamina to a marriage union.

The plan and purpose of this book is to direct individuals to the best and most reliable sourcebook on marriage,
the Bible. This work is offered with the conviction that
the Word of God contains every pertinent principle that
a husband and wife will need in order to make their marriage beautiful, exciting, and successful. It is here, in the
pages of the Bible, that they can find the understanding
and enlightenment they need to build an enduring, gratifying, marriage union. The format of this book is to search
out each and every scripture that pertains to husbands and
wives and the roles they must embrace.

Those who have chosen to castigate the Bible, and what it sets forth concerning marriage, will reject this book. They have the right to do so. On the other hand, those who choose to put on the mind of Christ and practice the firm and lasting marriage principles set forth in the Bible can and will enjoy a wonderful satisfying marriage union. In this book, references to Christian Believers will be capitalized to accentuate how outstanding and special they are. They will live on in eternity, so they deserve to be recognized for who they are. They are truly set apart from all others. Additionally, the words, "Holy Spirit," will appear in upper case letters when referring to God, who is " The Holy Spirit." When referring to the gift God has given those born-again, the words "holy spirit" will appear in lower case letters.

Having lived through two hurtful divorces, my third marriage is now in its 35th year. It is not without opportunities and challenges; however, my wife and I work at it with deliberate seriousness. We love each other deeply. We also love and respect God's Word and what it teaches about the union of marriage. The standard we share is that the Living Word of God provides the keys we need to keep our marriage working at its best.

Our calling and our duty as Christian marriage partners is to manifest the beauty and grace of a godly union. As we do so, our testimony to the eyes of the world will be "Look on us, and the life we live as husband and wife. Our marriage is patterned after the relationship we share with our Heavenly Father. So much of what we share with Him, we share with each other. Look on us, look on our marriage and you will see how we love and respect each other; how we are gracious and merciful to one another; how we forgive and forget; how we encourage, support, and fortify each other." Can you see it? Our marriage is a treasure that we share and a blessing to those who look upon us.

ACKNOWLEDGMENTS

M y sons, Charlie P. the III (Chuck), and Daniel Johnston, my mother, Ollie Johnston, and my friends, Dave Duris, and Joan Redemann, have all made this a better book by their helpful input and diligent critiquing. Their giving hearts have blessed my efforts with this book. My sister in Christ, Sharon L. Miller, has edited this book with her skillful ability. What an asset to have her help in the publication of this book.

My loving wife, Carol, stood by my side and faithfully supported the entire process of writing this book. She has corrected, clarified, simplified and improved the text of this book. As usual, she did all this with a joyful, giving heart. What a friend and helper she is! What a wife—My bride of over 35 years!

INTRODUCTION

I f marriage were always a wonderful bed of roses there would be no need for a book like this one and the hundreds of others that have been written over the years. Most marriages are far from the perfect "one flesh" union God designed marriage to be. However, we know from the description in Genesis, Adam and Eve were literally one flesh. They did not grow through a process to become one flesh, they were initially built to be one flesh. Adam declared that Eve is "bone of my bone and flesh of my flesh." (Gen. 2:23). Eve was in fact called woman because she was taken out of her husband's flesh and blood. The Biblical meaning of "one flesh" needs to be clearly understood because it is a foundational necessity for a marriage to flourish. Division between a husband and wife aggravates and frustrates their ability to complete each other.

The declaration of Genesis 2:24 is that future men and women choosing marriage are to become one flesh.

Genesis 2:24:
Therefore shall a man leave his father and his mother, and shall cleave unto his wife: and they shall be one flesh.

God Himself has established this one flesh standard. Men and women are individuals outside of the marriage union; however, in marriage the two of them are to become one flesh. So, becoming one in marriage is now a process. Obviously a couple must work together in harmony to achieve it.

The "book of all books", our Bible, has defined for us what marriage truly is to be. The need is that we learn to trust what it proclaims. It describes the beauty of marriage in the Garden of Eden but it also shows us the affect sin brought upon it. The effect of sin undermined Adam and Eve's marriage union. Their strife-free live together was hindered. The compatible relationship they had enjoyed with each other was broken. Genesis 3:16 clarifies the occasion of that change. Speaking to the woman God said:

"Thy desire shall be to thy husband, and he shall rule over thee."

The phrase, "Thy desire shall be to thy husband" is a difficult translation to understand. However, the scholarship of Susan T. Foh has provided the accuracy needed to understand this difficult phrase. This is the conclusion she reach in her article "What is the Woman's Desire?"printed in The Westminster Theological Journal 37(1974/75) p 383

> Contrary to the usual interpretations of commentators, the desire of the woman in Genesis 3:16 does not make the wife (more) submissive to her husband so that he may rule over her. Her desire is to

contend with him for leadership in their relationship. This desire is a result of and a just punishment for sin, but it is not God's decretive will [the intended order God first designed for Eve's marriage] for the woman. Consequently, the man must actively seek to rule his wife.

The impact of Eve's sin resulted in fracturing the harmony of the "one flesh" she had shared with Adam. She consequently began to rebel against her husband's headship position. Her "desire" changed from trusting Adam's leadership to challenging the authority of his leadership. Adam and Eve's punishment for sin led directly to conflict between them as husband and wife. They began to compete with each other. Eve tried to take Adam's leadership role and Adam began to rule over his wife in a dictatorial fashion. Strife and ruinous division had now entered their marriage union.

Husbands and wives have struggled in contentious marriages from Adam and Eve's day up to our own. Job's wife counseled him to curse God and die. Moses granted hard-hearted husbands the right to put away their wives by a bill of divorcement. Hard-hearted Pharisees sought for Jesus to justify the divorcement of their spouses. The Catholic Church has forced quarreling couples to remain united by the threat of excommunication. Statistics claim that almost 50% of every marriage fails here in the United States. A high percentage of the younger generation, in our day, ignore marriage vows and are living is so called "shacked-up" relationships.

So the question is: are husbands and wives without any remedy to the dilemma of a stressful, unhappy marriage? Must they remain locked into the contentious, decaying, patterns of marriage which have been practiced from Adam and Eve's day to our own? NO, NO! ABSOLUTELY NOT!

Though largely ignored the pathway to a harmonious, one-flesh marriage is clearly presented to husbands and wives in the Bible. God has certainly provided the means to recover from the tragedy of a contentious union. He has provided the pathway to marriage restoration. And His provision for marriage restoration is exactly what we seek out in the pages of this book. We are going to take a thorough look into the many Scriptures that teach us how to achieve a joyous, one-flesh, marriage. Among these are the seven New Testament Scriptures that ask a wife to submit to her husband and the motivation that will move her to do so. The cultural patterns of marriage in our day are at enmity with God's marriage plan. We are going to discover what enables a wonderful wife to withstand the intimidation against her trusting in the Word of God.

Much is required of husbands in the Biblical standard of marriage. He is to love his wife just as he loves himself; just as they are one flesh, not two. And you know that she is not always going to be so perfect is she? So, we are going to examine this requirement and others that need to be implemented in building an uplifting one-flesh marriage union. To be the head of his wife is first and foremost a spiritual position for a husband. As we shall see, his standing with and before God will vastly affect the quality of his leadership. If he is going to have real success in marriage he needs to reflect the glory of God in the way he lives before his wife! This is the challenging standard required of a Christian husband. Hallelujah, God's Word will teach him exactly how to do it.

Now let's get started - and with exciting expectations. Let's get rid of the strife in our marriage. Let's get rid of the conflict and hostility. Let's get ready to both receive and practice all that God designed marriage to be. Let's embrace the excellency of God's Word and learn to walk in the light of it. It is the truth of God's Word concerning marriage that will set us free.

CHAPTER 1

CONSIDERATIONS ABOUT
MARRIAGE

ᶜ∾ᵒ

WHAT MARRIAGE IS NOT

Throughout history, men and women have joined together in unions they have called marriage. However, what has been called marriage has constantly changed from one generation to the next. It has also differed from one culture to another. That which is called marriage today would not have been allowed by the 1950s generation. Nor would couples today allow what was practiced in the Civil War era. Cultures and customs have defined how marriage is perceived and practiced. Looking at marriage in history, it's easy to see that marriage principles and practices were not "set in stone;" they continually changed. Today, we don't expect a bride to bring a large dowry. Earlier generations would not have tolerated the dating practices of today. It would be easy to come to the conclusion that "marriage is as marriage does."

There are many modern-day matrimonial practices that veer away from the sum-and- substance of what God designed marriage to be. In a "trial marriage" arrangement, a couple agrees to live together without formalizing their relationship. This is a good example of veering away from the normal abiding love commitment required in traditional biblical marriage. Trial marriage couples claim that they are just waiting to see whether it is going to "work out." They are not willing to accept the duty to love each other even in difficult times. Their selfishness is plainly evident. They are behaving much like spoiled children who must have their own way.

The practice of a "co-equal marriage partnership" is another example of veering away from what God designed. In a co-equal marriage partnership there can be no single authority. Yes, the appealing idea of co-equal marriage sounds inviting, even very democratic. However, it is a sham devised by the wishful thinking of misguided individuals. "Fifty-fifty" marriages are impossible. They do not work. God vested the leadership of "loving authority" upon the husband and he remains responsible for his wife.

There are more graphic examples of how some husbands and wives have veered away in what they allow. The absurdity of some of the relationships men and women are sharing in marriages today qualifies them for "X-rated" viewing guidelines.[1] In so-called "open marriage," a couple agrees that each may have outside lovers. The term "swingers" refers to married couples engaging in extramarital sex together as a couple at organized gatherings. In "group marriage" there is no primary core-couple but all members are equally married to each other in the group.

The problem is that what millions of couples commonly practiced as marriage is not what God calls marriage. There is a very big discrepancy between the two. The shameful fighting and bickering between husbands and wives is not what God had in mind. Cruelty and abuse between husbands and wives is not what God had in mind. Manipulation and deceit between a man and a woman is not what God had in mind. Running home to Mama is not what God had in mind. Running around with the boys and snubbing a wife is not what God had in mind. Adultery is certainly not what God had in mind.

None of this anemic, misguided behavior has anything to do with God's design for matrimony. Nevertheless, this is often the behavior practiced between a husband and his wife. Actually, we could get more "graphic" about the wayward behavior of some married couples toward one another. Sexual infidelity by one or both partners; hatreds and animosities festering in their hearts; even the extreme of murder, all of these unbelievable kinds of behavior exists between men and women who call themselves husband and wife. The immorality of this behavior is self-evident. Some of it is even criminal. God certainly did not have criminal acts between a man and his bride in mind when He designed the union of marriage. Actually, the Word of God has a name for this kind of detestable behavior, and it is called sin.

The carnal, debasing, acts that have been practiced among many marriage partners certainly gives rise to some valid questioning. Who are the bride and groom that would consent to a union that brings such misery and heartache? After all, don't their marriage vows spell out devotion and faithfulness and commitment and love and support? How is it then that this kind of uncanny behavior gets into their union? After they promise "I do," what is it that goes so wrong later on down the road they are traveling together? This is what we need to discover. We need to see beyond the anemic marriage unions that are defined by broken promises and broken hearts. What we need to discover is the awesome possibilities that God built into a proper union, a marriage union of His making.

Just ahead, we are going to study the up-lifting way God designed marriage to function. Before we do so, while we are on the subject of what marriage is <u>not</u>, we must address homosexuality. Today some are calling homosexual unions a marriage. Men with men and women with women are "working that which is unseemly" and they are calling upon our society to grant them the status of a legitimate marriage relationship. These so-called "homosexual marriage unions" have become a striking example to us of how far out of bounds and desperate individuals have gotten with their lustful behavior.

Homosexuals are men and women who have opened up their lives to the practice of lewd sexual perversion. What they do among themselves is shameful; it's a despicable practice! The perversion of homosexuality is actually fostered by satanic influence, and can lead directly to devil spirit possession. The manipulating action of a devil-spirit can persuade an individual that it's okay to do it. The spirit blocks off the individual's mind to the unwholesome nature of homosexuality. It persuades the individual that they have "a bent," to the same sex and they just can't help it—it's beyond their control. All of this is, of course, ridiculous deception. The truth of the matter is that homosexuality remains sexual perversion, and God calls it by that name. The homosexuals who seek to justify their sordid lifestyle must do so by lying to themselves. They try in vain to negate what the Word of God has to say about this lascivious practice. The following verses tell us exactly what God has to say about men and women who practice this perversion.

Romans 1:24-28:
Wherefore God also gave them up to uncleanness through the lusts of their own hearts, to dishonour their own bodies between themselves: Who changed the truth of God into a lie, and worshipped and served the creature more than the Creator, who is blessed for ever. Amen.
For this cause God gave them up unto vile affections: for even their women did change the natural use into that which is against nature: And likewise also the men, leaving the natural use of the woman, burned in their lust one toward another; men with men working that which is unseemly, and receiving in themselves that recompence of their error which was meet.

> And even as they did not like to retain God in their knowledge, God gave them over to a reprobate mind, to do those things which are not convenient.

It is outrageously sad that our legislators and politicians nod and lightly accept the practice of homosexuality. But, it is obvious that God will not accept this shameful behavior. He condemns it and so must we! The repulsive idea that two people of the same sex can live together and form a marriage relationship is more than absurd, it's devilish. This whole topic of homosexual marriage is a startling example of how twisted people's logic has become. Nothing about this demeaning activity could ever serve as a foundation for a marriage relationship. Outrageous homosexual marriage unions are a testament to how far away from God's marriage plan some individuals have fallen. Marriage can never be a man with a man, or a woman with a woman. "Queer" is the term that was used to describe homosexual activity in the 1950s; it's a truthful description of the unsavory practice.

Deliverance from this sinful practice is available. God forgives sin! His outstretched hand of deliverance beckons to the men and women who have been ensnared by this lifestyle. They have only to grasp God's hand and His power will lift them up and give them the deliverance they need. They must first recognize that homosexuality is sin. They must put aside this practice and turn to God for forgiveness. The man or woman needs to take control of their thinking. They can, and must close off their minds to any acceptance of homosexuality. They must also abandon any further contact with practicing homosexuals. Fellowship with Christian Believers will strengthen their resolve; the warmth of God's people will encourage them. By the power of God they can be set completely free from the captive grasp of devil spirit control.

MARRIAGE IS MADE IN HEAVEN

Marriage has always been the structure upon which the stability of society rests. Do away with marriage and society, as we know it, will fall apart. Much of the confusion and heartache we witness in the world today can be traced directly to the astounding numbers of busted homes and marriages. Within society, the family unit remains the glue that holds us together. Much of the frontal attacks that we see upon the institution of marriage and family life is an attempt to destroy the fundamental order God designed for human existence. By the way, the government has no business trying to dictate rules and regulation about marriage. The government's real motive is to levy tax. The state did not institute marriage in the beginning; God did that. Marriage is an institution of God's making, and not that of a man. So in light of this reality, no one should be so surprised when the man-made counterfeit versions of it fail—and these versions are failing big time today! We have looked at some of these failures already. Again, what we have before us here is a discrepancy between what people commonly "call" marriage, and what God made marriage to be.

People simply do not have the capacity, by themselves, to figure out all that's involved in the marriage relationship.

Since it was not man who figured out the fundamentals of marriage we need to wake up and realize that God established them for us. We need to stop dragging our feet, and instead adopt and practice His plan; it's the only one that works.

> *Psalms 100:3:*
> Know ye that the Lord, He is God: it is he that hath made us, and not we ourselves; we are his people, and the sheep of his pasture.

God certainly knows us better than we know ourselves. He understands what we are capable of. In other words, He knows our capacities because He is the one who gave them to us. God designed marriage to meet specific human needs. His Word teaches us the depth of how these needs are going to be met. His instructions are specifically addressed to both a husband and a wife. The Word of God tells the husband how to be a loving husband and it tells the wife how to be an obedient wife. Every aspect of how marriage works is there for us to study, to learn and to carry out. It is by following these godly-designed precepts and judgments that a husband and a wife can build and enjoy a truly fulfilling marriage union. The union of marriage is made in heaven; and, when it is carried out here on earth, as God designed it, it works great. Who knows better than God?

God did not intend the twisted, anemic, version of marriage, which reflects hard hearts and ill wills. Marriage cannot work without the godly qualities of kindness, generosity, mercy, forgiveness and love. It is God's relationship with His people that have established the right pattern for a marriage union. His goodness, His long-suffering, His mercy, His forgiveness, His abiding love and patience are the outstanding qualities a husband and wife need to practice in order to bind themselves together. When we do it His way, our marriage will be a reflection of God's glory at work within us. What we need to understand is that God is the foundation upon which the union of marriage must rest. Who else could determine that a husband and wife must cleave to each other and separate themselves from Mom and Dad, or that a husband and wife are to become one flesh? Who else could determine that a husband is to love his wife as his own flesh, and that a wife is to submit to her husband? It had to be God and God alone.

It was God who gave marriage its identity; He alone separated it out from among all other human relationships. Because He did so, the people of this world can now look upon its uniqueness. When marriage is fulfilled the way God intended, on-lookers are able to gaze upon godly husbands and wives who are faithfully living out their marriage vows. From godly Christian unions, the people of this world can learn about the depth of God's goodness, His tenderness, His far-reaching care and love. This is true because God designed marriage to be a reflection of His own nature. When people look upon a Christian marriage they should get a tremendous demonstration of how God behaves toward all people. When a Christian man and woman come together in matrimony they have the opportunity, and also the privilege, to demonstrate the love of

God that lives within them. As they show their love to each other the people of this erring world can be uplifted by the testimony of their wonderful marriage.

We know that our Lord Jesus Christ was the perfect portrayal of God; he always did the will of his Heavenly Father. The wonderful ministry of Jesus Christ has taught us so much about God. His life reflected his Heavenly Father to the world. If you want to know what God is like, just look at the life of our Lord Jesus Christ. A Christian marriage can, and must, reflect the God in Christ who lives within that union. A husband and wife who are born-again of God's spirit certainly have the ability to show forth the "excellency" of God's nature in the way they behave toward each other. Truthfully, this is the high calling of their marriage union. They are a couple bound together for a lifetime. They are born-again of God's spirit; they have the power of God living within them. Because they are a son and a daughter of God, bound together in marriage, they can proclaim to the world, "Go ahead, look on us; look on our marriage union. We seek to behave like our Heavenly Father; yes, we love Him, we serve Him, we thank Him, we want to be like Him. Look on our marriage and learn about our God's goodness, His grace, His mercy, His peace and His forgiveness. We are followers of God as dear children.

Thoughtfulness, tenderness, kindness, consideration, respect, care and concern, compassion, honor, grace, mercy and loving charity are some of the fruits of our godly marriage union."

Philippians 4:8-9:
Finally, brethren, whatsoever things are true, whatsoever things are honest, whatsoever things are
just, whatsoever things are pure, whatsoever things
are lovely, whatsoever things are of good report; if
there be any virtue, and if there be any praise, think
on these things. Those things, which ye have both
learned, and received, and heard, and seen in me,
do: and the God of peace shall be with you.

Now, this Christian couple may not get it right every day and
on every occasion because learning and growing and matur-
ing are needful. After all, they are imperfect people, and
they are living in physically decaying bodies, and the god of
this world continues to lay his snares and temptations before
them. However, it is absolutely true that the power of God
resides within them. As their minds are renewed to that power
and they manifest its presence in their daily lives, the people
of this world will take notice. They will see in this Christian
husband and wife what God has intended marriage to be.
They will see a dynamic union between a Christian husband
and wife that is a reflection of their Heavenly Father and the
fellowship they share with Him, and with each other.

BE FRUITFUL AND MULTIPLY

If we are going to know how marriage got its start, we need to
take a look at the first one. The first marriage was certainly
unique. Adam's bride was made out of his own flesh. She
was built from the material taken out from behind his rib.
The two of them were literally of one flesh. Brides today are

11

not taken out from behind their husband's rib, but the two do become one flesh in marriage. Adam and Eve's Maker united them in marriage— they became husband and wife.

Genesis 2:23:
And Adam said, this is now bone of my bones and flesh of my flesh: she shall be called woman, because she was taken out of man.

Genesis 1:28a:
And God blessed them, and God said unto them, Be fruitful, and multiply, and replenish the earth, and subdue it.

God brought Eve to Adam and He "blessed them together" in their union. They were told to be fruitful and multiply and thereby populate the earth. Throughout the course of the Old Testament there was a great deal of emphasis placed upon the importance of producing children—the larger the family, the better. Men and women were prideful about the number of offspring they could produce. For example, both Abraham and his grandson, Jacob, rejoiced at the promise of God that He would multiply their offspring as the stars of heaven, and as the sand by the seashore. God chose the union of marriage as the means by which He would populate the planet. By the New Testament era, the earth had been populated twice, once before the flood in the days of Noah, and once again after it.

Yes, God had a divine purpose in mind when He made Adam and Eve. God made them to share companionship with Him and with each other. He gave them freedom of will so that they might choose to love and obey Him in response to His love and goodness. (God is love; and we love Him because He first loved us, I John 4:19). It is important to recognize that when God created Adam and Eve, He gave them a body, a soul, and a spirit; that is how they were made. Spirit life was created within them—it was a part of their nature. Since God is spirit they were able to perceive God spiritually. They walked and talked with God and He with them; they shared companionship with each other. However, disobedience to the Word of God destroyed Adam and Eve's spiritual nature. They lost their spiritual nature; it died within them. Consequently they lost the connection they had enjoyed with God.

The restoration of man's SPIRITUAL nature would come about through the accomplished works of Jesus Christ. It was by the fruit of marriage that the Savior of the World, the Lord Jesus Christ, was born in Bethlehem. Through the union of marriage, within each succeeding generation, the lineage of Jesus Christ developed. Eve rejoiced with the birth of her first son. She mistakenly thought that she had given birth to the promised seed when Cain was born (Genesis 4:1).

By the day of the prophet Malachi, a few generations before the birth of Christ, Judaean priests were dealing deceitfully with their wives. They were not remaining faithful to their marriage covenant promises. They were undermining their marriage covenants by divorcing their wives. In the verses that follow, we can see how God taught these erring husbands a few aspects about marriage they needed to understand.

13

Malachi 2:14b-15:
Because the Lord hath been witness between thee and the wife of thy youth, against whom thou hast dealt treacherously: yet is she thy companion, and the wife of thy covenant. And did not he make one? Yet had he the residue of the spirit. And wherefore one? That he might seek a godly seed. Therefore take heed to your spirit, and let none deal treacherously [deceitfully] against the wife of his youth.

Yes, God had made a man and his wife to become one in the lifetime commitment of marriage. The phrase "yet had he the residue of the spirit" teaches us that God had plenty of power. He chose the union of marriage to be the means by which He would bring about the birth of Jesus Christ—a godly seed. If He had wanted to do it another way He had the power to do so; but marriage was the way He chose. He made marriage a lifetime commitment for a purpose. The phrase "that he might seek a godly seed" teaches us the great spiritual significance that is wrapped up within the bond of marriage. It took husbands and wives that would faithfully honor their marriage covenants to bring about the birth of Jesus Christ. When we stop and think about the husbands and wives who are listed in the ancestral lineage of Jesus Christ, we can begin to understand that by staying put in their marriage unions they became vital parts of all that was required to produce the birth of Jesus Christ.

Think about the wonderful marriage union of Joseph and Mary—how tremendous it was. Joseph was a just man. He mistakenly thought Mary had breached their union by committing adultery. Even in this horrific development he was willing to protect Mary from the consequences of public condemnation. What a loving, faithful, man he was. He willingly carried out exactly what God asked him to do. He willingly took upon himself the full responsibility of caring for, and raising up, the only begotten Son of God. Take a look at Mary's great humility of heart. Her response to, the angel, Gabriel's words were, "behold the handmaid of the Lord, be it unto me according to thy word"(Luke 1:38). Mary's spirit rejoiced in God, her Savior. The marriage union of Joseph and Mary was exactly what God needed to facilitate the birth of Jesus Christ, the Savior of the world. The loving devotion Joseph and Mary had for each other, and their faithfulness to obey God, set the stage for the birth of the promised Messiah, Jesus Christ. It was through his birth and his accomplished works—a sinless life, his sacrificial death, his resurrection, and his ascension, that men and women are now, once again, able to regain a spiritual nature. By the new birth we become born-again of God's spirit. (Later we are going to study some additional spiritual aspects of marriage.)

Husbands here in the book of Malachi had lost sight of the godly design of marriage. God asked them to "take heed to your spirit." In other words, what was this sour frame-of-mind that motivated you to break your marriage covenants and put away your wives? These husbands needed to scrutinize their thinking and change their behavior. It was before God they had promised, by a marriage covenant, to provide companionship to their wives for the rest of their days. They needed to honor what they had sworn before God to do. They also needed to wake up to the awesome possibility that their marriage union might be instrumental in bringing forth the promised Messiah, the Savior of the World.

It is vital that we understand that marriage is something God designed. We must <u>not</u> lose sight of this important reality. In the pages that follow we will attempt to cover every essential aspect of what God teaches us about marriage. Farther along in this study we will be taking an in-depth look at the significance of the marriage covenant, and the part companionship plays in the marriage union. Among the many other topics that we are going to study, we will also be looking at the horrific subject of divorce.

WITNESSES TO THE WORLD

The emphasis in the New Testament has changed from populating the world and the birth of the promised Messiah, to teaching men and women how to become born-again of God's spirit. Now, in our day, the spiritual natures of men and women can be reclaimed. The ministry of our Lord Jesus Christ completed every aspect of that which was needed to restore the spiritual nature of men and women. He paid the price for our sins. He's given us hope and peace with God. He has made it available for men and women to regain their spiritual standing before God. Now they can become born-again of God's spirit.

John 3:16:
For God so loved the world, that he gave his only begotten Son, that whosoever believeth in him should not perish, but have everlasting life.

Whosoever believes in their heart that God raised Jesus Christ from the dead, and makes him the Lord of their life, will become born-again of God's spirit. Praise God! By doing so they will have gained a spiritual connection with God. After we become born-again of God's spirit, our goal in life is no longer to please ourselves. Our goal is to please our Lord and Savior, who laid down his life that we might have "fullness of life." We have become followers of the Lord Jesus Christ, and he has given us a work to do. The Great Commission calls for men and women of the church age, first and foremost, to be witnesses of the Lord Jesus Christ. Jesus did not encourage the church to go forth and populate the world; he asked that we be witnesses to the world. As stated previously, our marriage relationships are to be a testimony to the eyes of a lost and dying world.

Mark 16:15:
And he said unto them, go ye into all the world and preach the gospel to every creature.

The great Apostle Paul reflects this same emphasis in his second letter to the Corinthian church.

II Corinthians 5:19-20:
To wit [to know] that God was in Christ reconciling the world unto Himself not imputing their trespasses unto them, and hath committed unto us the word of reconciliation. Now then we are ambassadors for Christ, as though God did beseech you by us, we pray you in Christ stead, be ye reconciled to God.

Life's highest calling is from God. First and foremost, we are called to serve Him. We do this by the way we choose to live before Him. Because we answer to Him, we need to choose a lifestyle that will enable us to fulfill the work He has given us to do. He has made us ambassadors for the Lord Jesus Christ. This means that we are to remain faithful witnesses of our Lord and Savior. It's true that the work we do to support ourselves financially helps to keep body and soul together. Most all of us are engaged in some kind of employment or business. However, a bigger vocation than that of our secular job is our heavenly vocation.

If we are thinking spiritually, it's not just OUR work, it's God's work we need to be about. God's work ranks even higher in importance than how we earn our living. The important question we need to answer, as individuals is, "How can I best do the work He has given me to do and faithfully fulfill my calling?" Jesus has set before us a tremendous example of this. After three days of searching Joseph and Mary found their son, Jesus, setting in the temple asking and answering questions about his Heavenly Father's Word. His parents questioned his behavior; he had failed to leave with them at the appointed time to return home together to Galilee. His answer to them was, "I must be about my Father's business." He answered so perfectly, even though he was only 12 years old at that time. The driving force in his young mind and heart was to serve his Heavenly Father. He needed to be about his Father's business, and so must we! We too need to be about our Heavenly Father's business.

DO YOU REALLY NEED A MATE?

What an important question to answer, one of the biggest an individual will need to decide upon while living on this Earth. Culturally, for generations we have been taught that marriage is the right thing to do. When you grow up you get married and have kids. That's the image that was laid before us in days gone by. However, from the biblical perspective of I Corinthians: 7, getting married may not be the best thing to do. In this section of the Bible we have a broad perspective of life laid before us. Here we are taught that choosing marriage for one's self should be based upon need. So then, a legitimate need to be married is the right standard. It is this need that should govern one's decision. So marriage might not be the right decision for some individuals.

The apostle Paul encouraged individuals in the Corinthian church to stay put in their current lifestyle. We're going to look at three important verses of Scripture from Corinthians Chapter 7: they will give us the spiritual perspective concerning a decision to marry.

Verse 17 a:
But as God hath distributed to every man, as the Lord hath called everyone, so let him walk.

Verse 20:
Let every man abide in the same calling where in he was called.

Verse 25:
Brethren, let every man, wherein he is called, therein abide with God.

These three Scriptures are referring to the future direction of an individual's life after he or she first becomes born-again of God's spirit. How can they best live before God and serve Him, now that they are Christian Believers? So then, when a man or a woman has become born again of God's spirit, and they have no pressing need for marriage, the better choice for them is to remain single. The reason for this is that the responsibilities and obligations of being married will require a great deal of their time and energies. The focus of their activities in life will change after marriage. In marriage they are going to be thinking about houses, cars children, bank accounts and all that's involved in pleasing that husband or that wife. By remaining single their time and their energy can be directed toward the fulfillment of their unique calling; their unique ministry of witnessing to men and women concerning the hope alive within them. They will be able to travel lighter in life. They can devote much more of their time and effort into ministering "the bread of life" to the people of this world. It's the focus of their lives that is the key consideration.

I Corinthians 7: 32-33:
But I would have you without carefulness [anxiety]. He that is unmarried, careth for the things that belong to the Lord, how he may please the Lord, but he that is married careth for the things that are of the world, how he may please his wife.

What we need to see about this important question of marriage is the big picture—a perspective that includes the totality of our lives in relationship to our Christian calling. This broader prospective of life enables us to understand that we are "bought with a price" by the shed blood of Jesus Christ, our living Lord and Savior. We are not our own any longer; we are called to serve God. Now in the face of this great reality, how can we be our best for Him? This is what we really need to answer. If there is no necessity, if there is not a genuine need for marriage, then the better decision is not to get married. Marriage, just for the sake of marriage, is not the right decision. What is the best way to serve my Lord? The honest answer to this important question will bring about the right decision.

A PROPER GIFT

Before God made Eve, Adam lived alone upon the face of the earth. Adam's life took on a new dimension with the presence of a woman. God designed this woman to be a wonderful companion for His man. The general rule outlined for us in Genesis 2:18 is clear, "it is not good that the man should be alone." God gave this rule; however, He did make at least one exception to it. We know this is true because a New Testament record reveals it. The apostle Paul describes this exception to the general rule.

Corinthians 7:7-8:
For I would that all men were even as I myself. But every man hath his proper gift of God, one after this manner, and another after that. I say therefore to

the unmarried and widows, it is good for them if they abide even as I.

The apostle Paul may have had a wife at one time. No one knows for certain.

Nevertheless, he was living the life of a single man when writing this epistle to the Corinthian Church. He certainly served God without a wife from the date of his Damascus Road conversion until his death. Because of the impending work of his ministry he continued to serve without a wife. The pressing work of his calling consumed his time and his life's energies. Marriage for Paul would have been a distraction. The tremendous obstacles he faced in carrying the gospel message to a Gentile world would have made marriage very difficult for him.

Married life for a "Mrs. John The Baptist" would have been extremely difficult. Can you imagine how she would have managed living in the Judean wilderness for all those years? Locus and wild honey may not have met her taste requirements. John the Baptist did not need the companionship of a wife. He was one of many whom Paul described as having been given a "proper gift." God has gifted certain individuals with the capacity to serve without the companionship of a wife or a husband. Jesus referred to these gifted individuals.

Matthew 19:12:
For there are some eunuchs, which were so born from their mother's womb: and there are some eunuchs, which were made eunuchs of men: and

there be eunuchs, which have made themselves
eunuchs for the kingdom of heaven's sake. He that
is able to receive it, let him receive it.

There are certain individuals, whom God has called to serve
in this capacity—without marriage. He has given them
the ability to do so. These gifted individuals manage fine
without the companionship of a mate. They are able to
function without loneliness. They can confidently remain
single because they have a greater priority than marriage.
This was true of the Apostle Paul and John the Baptist. It is
also true of some men and women today. These wonderful
single men and women get their gratification and satisfaction from the work of ministering to the body of Christ.
This is how their needs are met; and, they should be honored for their calling and the work they do.

History has also shown us that there are times and situations in which marriage must become a secondary consideration. An example of this can be seen by looking at
how Jesus referred to life in the days of Noah before the
flood. He explained that they were marrying and being
given in marriage. But to what end? Suddenly, without
warning, they all perished in one day. Jesus also warned
his disciples that in the days ahead great destruction would
come upon the city of Jerusalem and the nation of Judah.
That came to pass, 40 years later, when the mighty Roman
army swept across Judea. They destroyed their cities, and
crucified millions of men and women. In the verse below
the Apostle Paul, quite possibly, is referring to that impending doom which lay ahead for most all Judeans. Whatever

the distress, it was demanding enough to put serious strains upon normal marriage relationships.

> *I Corinthians 7:26-27:*
> I suppose therefore that this is good for the present distress, I say, that it is good for a man so to be. Art thou bound unto a wife? seek not to be loosed. Art thou loosed from a wife? seek not a wife. But and if thou marry, thou hast not sinned; and if a virgin marry, she hath not sinned. Nevertheless such shall have trouble in the flesh: but I spare you.

Marriage in the face of such great upheaval could be a very serious handicap. Actually, married couples have tremendous strains put upon their union in times of war and separation. Oh, how a wife lives in such great apprehension when her husband is on the front lines of a battlefield. And, how a man longs for his wife and children who may be thousands of miles away.

In the verses that follow Paul elevates his teaching beyond the issue of marriage. Here his view is of eternity. From the standpoint of our lives in eternity, the years we live on earth are short indeed.

> *I Corinthians 7:29-31:*
> But this I say, brethren, the time is short: it remaineth, that both they that have wives be as though they had none; And they that weep, as though they wept not; and they that rejoice, as though they rejoiced not;

and they that buy, as though they possessed not;
And they that use this world, as not abusing it: for
the fashion of this world passeth away.

Considerations of marriage, and other social relationships
are temporal. Considerations of business and vocations
and possessions are also temporal. All of these are going to
pass away. The fashion of this world will change.

I Corinthians 3:11-14:
For other foundation can no man lay than that is
laid, which is Jesus Christ. Now if any man build
upon this foundation gold, silver, precious stones,
wood, hay, stubble; Every man's work shall be made
manifest: for the day shall declare it because it shall
be revealed by fire; and the fire shall try every man's
work of what sort it is. If any man's work abide which
he hath built thereupon, he shall receive a reward.

If we are spiritually minded the decisions we make regarding
marriage, business, social relationships, and any other
earthly endeavor, needs to be predicated upon those values
that will endure in eternity. We need to give ourselves
to works that will abide. The fundamental reality
is that we are sons and daughters of God. We are born-
again of His spirit. And, our lives must be built upon the
foundation Jesus Christ has laid for us. Our work is to do
his works. Our lifestyle needs to be fashioned in such a
way that our works will last even after this Old World has
passed away.

There are indeed many that will need to be married. The need of companionship is paramount in their hearts and lives. Marriage is definitely the right decision for them. However, we need to remember that there are some that can serve God best living the single life. Their need for companionship can be met outside of a marriage union. They can get really excited about serving God in ways a married couple could never enjoy. It also has a great deal to do with sexual needs and self-discipline. Sexual passions are greater for some than for others.

This decision about marriage is not a question of right or wrong; instead, it's simply a question of need or the lack thereof. In this category, it's just that some have better self-control sexually than others. Each one has their God-given ability. Those who are content to live their lives without a husband or a wife should not bow to undo pressure from their families to get married. Parents might like to have grandchildren, but they can get along just fine without them. Neither should undue pressure from well-meaning friends move a man or a woman into marriage. Those individuals who have established in their hearts that they do not need a marriage partner should stay put with that decision. Having control over their own desires and not being forced by sexual necessity to choose a marriage partner, they "do well" to stay just as they are—single. In the same way that it's better to stay single, if there is no pressing sexual need to marry, it's best for those who burn with sexual passion, and a longing for companionship with the opposite sex, to marry.

SEXUAL NEEDS

I Corinthians 7:9:
But if they cannot contain, let them marry: for it is better to marry than to burn.

The "to burn" phrase is a reference to sexual passion. If you're getting married so you can enjoy sex you're getting married for a very good reason. One important reason for getting married is sexual gratification. Morally, and biblically speaking, marriage is the RIGHT way to satisfy sexual passions. It is a legitimate reason for marriage. In fact, that is the way God designed it. Most of us have a healthy sexual appetite. God wanted us to have our sexual nature; that's why He put the need for sexual fulfillment within us. The human race might die out without sexual attraction between men and women. The sexual passions of an individual need to be met if they are going to be effective in the way they live. However, sexual needs are to be met in the bed of a wife or a husband, and not the bed of a casual acquaintance, or any other individual. God has provided the framework of marriage to meet the sexual needs of men and women.

I Corinthians 7:1-2:
Now concerning the things whereof ye wrote unto me: It is good for a man not to touch a woman. Nevertheless, to avoid fornication, let every man have his own wife, and let every woman have her own husband.

The word "touch" is a reference to touching in a sexual manner. Some women can be aroused sexually by stroking and cuddling. This verse is teaching us that it is not good to arouse her sexual passion, which could lead to sexual intercourse outside of marriage. Sadly, today's generation is being taught that casual sexual intercourse, outside of marriage, is acceptable. Sex between unmarried couples is even portrayed to be normal. You and I see this lifestyle portrayed before us constantly as we view television and movies. One of the research groups that tries to measure marriage trends reported that in 1977 one million couples were living together (cohabiting) outside of marriage. By 2007 the number had increased up to over six million. Pew Research conducts this kind of polling.[2] Today this number is up by several million more. (This is the one and only reference to polling you are going to see in this book, "Praise God!") Personally, you may know of singles that are involved sexually. You may have friends and acquaintances that are living together in this manner outside of a marriage relationship. It's sad to say but they are not being confronted by society. They are openly practicing fornication (sexual sin) without shame or remorse. They have tossed what God says about marriage to one side. In defiance of God's Word, and in the faces of their parents and acquaintances, they have set up their radical, unwholesome, lifestyle. Despite its widespread practice, intercourse between the unmarried has serious ramifications.

In case you have not noticed, just take a look around you at how we are constantly bombarded by sexual enticements. Television commercials are put together with the belief that, "sex sells." When we watch television we see sex, sex, sex and more sex. Of course, television and the entertainment world have a great bearing upon our cultural values. The teasing allurements of easy sex, hot sex, delicious sex, sex anywhere, anytime, with whomever, is laid out before us and we are encouraged to participate. It is no wonder people's sexual passions are stirred up. People's sexual passions were also being stirred up in the city of Corinth (the first century church to which Paul was writing). Perhaps people's sexual passions have been stirred up throughout history. This is not going to change. In light of this, the man or woman who cannot "sexually contain" should seek marriage. There is no need for them to be enticements, tricked and deceived into the practice of sexual immorality. The sexual values of our society are far below the standard God approves. The Word of God teaches us to "avoid" fornication. God has given us the proper way to enjoy sexual gratification. True sexual fulfillment is to be enjoyed between a husband and his wife.

Joseph, Jacob's son, knew how to stay out of sexual trouble (Genesis 39:7-12). His wisdom to flee from the enticements of Potiphar's wife is an excellent example of how to respond to sexual temptations. Day by day, Potiphar's wife asked Joseph to lay down and have sex with her while her husband was away. Day by day, she enticed him. Joseph was not going to have any part of that. He knew that doing so would betray his master's trust. More importantly, it would be sinning against his God. He didn't "horse around;" he didn't flirt; and he didn't give into the temptation. His action was to flee. He got out of there. He got out of that situation. What a great decision he made that day, and what a wonderful example for us to follow. We need to stay away from those situations that might arouse our sexual appetites and lead to fornication (sexual sin). Get out of there, don't hang around any environment which stirs-up elicit sexual passions. The loss of honor, the loss of health, and the loss of finances, are some of the painful fruits of fornication. Sexual sin is like any other sin, there is an exacting penalty to be paid.

I Corinthians 6:18:
Flee fortification. Every sin that a man doeth is without the body; but he that committeth fornication sinneth against his own body.

Sexually transmitted diseases work against the body and they are often times the hidden cost of fornication. Gonorrhea, syphilis, herpes, and HIV can be transmitted to the third and fourth generations. It is certainly against our own body when the power and influence of the spirit of God within us is effectively blocked by such behavior. We are not to allow sin to reign in our bodies, that we should obey it, in the lust thereof (Romans 6:12). We are men and women born-again of God's spirit. We are members of the body of Christ. We do not physically join our bodies together by sexual intercourse with another's spouse, or the unmarried, or whores, or prostitutes.

I Corinthians 6:15b-17:
Shall I then take the members of Christ, and make them the members of an harlot? God forbid. What?

know ye not that he which is joined to an harlot is one body? For two, saith he, shall be one flesh. But he that is joined unto the Lord is one spirit.

The ultimate decision we must make in this matter is whose word are we going to obey? Will we obey the voice of what our sick, fleeting, culture teaches is okay; or will we give proper credence to what God teaches in His wonderful Word? God's Word is the right choice; it teaches how sexual intercourse is to be practiced. Our Christian calling must remain our highest priority in life. "We are in this world but we are not of this world." Our standards must be based upon lasting and eternal spiritual values. Our calling is to live our lives in sanctification and honor. We refuse to accept the flaky standards of a modern-day loose-minded society—much of what it allows is repulsive. We live a much higher standard than, "if it feels good do it;" or, "everybody's doing it," etc. We just need to trust what God has to say about this subject. This is why we avoid fornication. Our aim is to please Him by living according to the standard of His Word. God knows best!

I Thessalonians 4:3-8:
For this is the will of God, even your sanctification, that ye should abstain from fornication: That every one of you should know how to possess his vessel in sanctification and honour;
Not in the lust of concupiscence, even as the Gentiles which know not God: That no man go beyond and defraud his brother in any matter: because that the Lord is the avenger of all such, as we also have

forewarned you and testified. For God hath not called us unto uncleanness, but unto holiness. He therefore that despiseth, despiseth not man, but God, who hath also given unto us his holy Spirit.

Sanctification and fornication cannot travel the same road together. As Christian Believers we are to present our bodies to God as living sacrifices; this is our religious duty (Romans 12). This is, after all, a major requirement of our sanctification. The command is that we are to abstain from fornication, and this is what we must do. We were not made to live for sexual satisfaction—we were created to live for the Lord! This word "abstain" means that we hold ourselves back from unbridled passions. We will not be swept away by our emotions. We will not allow our feelings to control us by leading us astray; we keep our feelings in check. This is how we are able to maintain peaceful minds that are free of guilt, condemnation and embarrassment.

Living our lives under the shelter of what God ask us to do pays big dividends. It also keeps us free from the snare of sin. Obeying God keeps us peaceful on the inside. It's absolutely worth it to do it God's way! We do not obey the, "seemingly sweet" enticement of lust. No matter how loudly lust calls, it should not be answered. What it has to offer is irrelevant to our lives.

Romans 8:5-6:
For they that are after the flesh do mind the things of the flesh; but they that are after the Spirit the

things of the Spirit. For to be carnally minded is death; but to be spiritually minded is life and peace.

We need to guard our hearts from the mind of the flesh. Just like our Lord Jesus Christ, we keep our minds focused on the joy that is set before us. In the end, the greatest joy and pleasure we will ever know will come from having pleased our Heavenly Father. God has given us holy spirit; we are men and women who are born-again by His power and grace. We do not walk in this life by the mind of the flesh; we are to discipline our minds to walk in the power of the spirit God has given us.

There are many other passages in the Bible that deal with the subject of fornication. Some that you might want to consult are: Matthew 5:32;15:19; Mark 7:21; Romans 1:29; I Corinthians 5:1; 6:13; II Corinthians 12:21; Galatians 5:19; Ephesians 5:3; Colossians 3:5; and Proverbs chapters 5 and 6.

SEXUAL DUTY

Sex is not only an enjoyable fulfillment between a man and his wife, it is also a duty— married couples are to meet each other's sexual needs. We are taught to lovingly function in that capacity with our mate.

I Corinthians 7:3-4:
Let the husband render unto the wife due benevolence: and likewise also the wife unto the husband. The wife hath not power of her own body, but the

husband: and likewise also the husband hath not power of his own body, but the wife.

Headaches, and tiredness, and other such made-up excuses do not do away with the sexual duty that needs to be fulfilled by marriage partners. The words, "render due benevolence," refer to the necessity of both a husband and a wife lovingly satisfying the sexual passions of each other. They are to share their bodies sexually with each other. Ideally, the "hot love" of the honeymoon needs to linger on throughout the years of marriage. Couples can work this lofty goal together by planning, thoughtfulness, and imagination. Then the duty is not drudgery but instead it becomes a wonderful fulfillment of their sexual passions for one another. A common statement you may have heard is that "sex starts at the breakfast table." That's a good place to start being real sweet on each other. It surely makes sense that kindness, tenderness, and mutual respect for each other throughout the day, sets the tone and develops the mood for enjoyable sex. When hearts are joined together in understanding, and harmony of purpose, and depth of love, the stage is set. Sexual intercourse can then become a joyful climatic fulfillment for both.

In the marriage relationship, the sexual needs of a husband are to be met by his wife and the sexual needs of a wife are to be met by her husband. Masturbation is a poor substitute for the sexual enjoyment they can bring to one another. The husband has the capacity to bring sexual fulfillment to his wife. He has the right equipment to do so. His sex organs are so designed that he is able to supply the sexual enjoyment and satisfaction his wife needs. The same is true of her. She is built with the capacity to supply sexual enjoyment and fulfillment for her husband. Her sex organs are constructed in just the right manner to do so. (God is so smart!) As the husband and wife lovingly give of themselves to each other, their sexual passions are going to be fulfilled. Together they can, and should, cultivate an exciting sex life; putting each other's needs first will produce the sexual gratification they both are seeking. Through tenderness, open honesty, and selfless giving, the sexual enjoyment and satisfaction they bring to each other can grow through the years of their marriage. Imagination, experimentation, and experience are good teachers.

CHAPTER 2

CHOOSING A MATE, WHO NOT TO MARRY

୧∿ଚ

UNEQUALLY YOKED

This is a good place to consider what the Bible teaches concerning being unequally yoked together with unbelievers. "Unequally yoked" would be like harnessing a horse and a cow together for the purpose of pulling a plow. It's not going to work well because they're not going to pull together as a team. Throughout the pages of the Old Testament, God warned the nation of Israel not to marry the pagan people who surrounded their borders. They were not to become unequally yoked in marriage with God-rejecting people. To do so would corrupt their lives, leading them to adopt pagan values and practices. King Solomon is a good example of a man who ignored this warning. He married pagan (God-rejecting) women from among many idolatrous nations.

I Kings 11:4:
For, it came to pass, when Solomon was old, that his wives turned away his heart after other gods: and his heart was not perfect with the Lord his God, as was the heart of David his father.

Giving in to the idolatrous mentality of his pagan wives was a big mistake. The bigger mistake Solomon made, first off, is that he ignored what God said. The Word of God said, DO NOT DO IT. Do not marry pagan women. He did so anyway, and He became the big-time loser for having done so. Because of the evil, idolatrous, influence of his pagan wives, King Solomon turned away from God. He knelt down and worshipped vicious pagan idols. His turning away from God led directly to the loss of his kingdom. His son, Rehoboam, inherited only a small fraction of the vast kingdom Israel had once been. A tremendous loss!

By contrast, a good example of a man who understood the dynamic importance of marriage between like-minded Believers was the patriarch Abraham. Abraham lived among idolatrous tribes in the land of Canaan. He saw their dark evil ways. When it was time for his son Isaac to take a bride, Abraham instructed his eldest servant, Eliezer, not to take a wife for his son from among the daughters of the idolatrous Canaanites. Instead, Abraham sent his servant, by camel, hundreds and hundreds of miles, to find a suitable wife for his son. His servant traveled to the distant land of Abraham's kindred. There his servant was to find a wife for Isaac—one who worshiped the God of Abraham, the true God of heaven and earth. God blessed that long trip of Abraham's servant. He successfully brought back a very beautiful, God-loving woman, whose name was Rebekah. She was a beautiful young woman who had godly standards and values built into the fabric of her life. She became Isaac's bride. Abraham's judgment to avoid taking a pagan wife for his son Isaac showed the soundness of his wisdom. He wanted the best for his son.

GOD ALWAYS KNOWS BEST

The victory for us in this matter of choosing a mate is to simply trust what God says. Sure rewards will always come by having done so. God's Word is designed to be our help and our stay. His commandments are not burdensome. God does His best to keep us out of life's pitfalls. The freedom of will He has given to us puts the ball in our court, so to speak. We must make the right choices. An essential key to a lasting, healthy, marriage is to marry a like-minded believing partner, one who loves God and the truth of His Word. Those who give in to the enticement of a "Hot Chick" or a "Sweet Mama" or a "Big Hunk," or any other flaky standard in choosing a mate, are headed for a turbulent future. Their lives are going to have cross-purposes. When they begin to experience the bitterness that comes from discord and strife, maybe they ought not to be so surprised—eventually the discord will come! A passage in the New Testament gets right to the heart and guts of this issue. What you chose to rub up against will rub off on you.

I Corinthians 15:33 (The Amplified Bible):
Do not be so deceived and misled! Evil companionship (communion, associations) corrupt and
deprave, good manners and morals, and character.[3]

Biblical teachings that instruct us not to marry the unbelieving ought to register in our thinking. The following
Scripture is the important standard of the New Testament
Church. It is the standard of light that we must trust because
we are living in a world of darkness. These instructions
need to register with us like a huge neon stop sign that
flashes, "STOP, DON'T DO IT." There can be no mistak-
ing what the Bible teaches concerning this important issue.
Its teaching is perfectly clear.

II Corinthians 6:14-18:
Be ye not unequally yoked together with unbelievers: for what fellowship hath righteousness with
unrighteousness? And what communion hath light
with darkness?
And what concord hath Christ with Belial? or what
part hath he that believeth With an infidel?
And what agreement hath the temple of God with
idols? for ye are the temple of the living God; as God
hath said, I will dwell in them, and walk in them; and
I will be their God, and they shall be my people.
Wherefore come out from among them, and be ye
separate, saith the Lord, and touch not the unclean
thing; and I will receive you.
And will be a Father unto you, and ye shall be my
sons and daughters, saith the Lord Almighty.

To be yoked together in marriage with a mate who rejects God and His Word is folly. A wise man or woman will stay away from it! 99% of the time such a lopsided marriage is going to be a mess that no one would knowingly choose to live within. You may think he is the "Salt of the Earth," or she is "God's Gift to Mankind" initially when you obviously know so little about them. It is certainly not wise to magnify a few good qualities that a potential mate may have out of all proportion. Remember that it takes a dark heart to reject our loving Heavenly Father. The standard by which you choose a mate needs to be rooted in the certainty and clarity of what God's Word proclaims. Its logic is ironclad— God certainly knows best about this matter of choosing a marriage partner. It is up to us to prove the uniqueness of our sanctification by our associations.

LACKING A SURE FOUNDATION

Without the spirit of God living within them, men and women are simply body and soul creatures. They have a mental and physical capacity, but they remain devoid of spiritual understanding. Because they block out the presence of God's spirit in their lives they lack stability. They are guided by the wisdom of men—or maybe by the lack of it. Consequently, in decision-making they flip-flop around, day by day, and year by year. They will constantly be changing their belief system. They will not stay put in that which they believe is right or wrong, good or bad. Because they are blinded to the spiritual realities of God they will make hit-and-miss decisions. Hits and misses over the eternal issues of life are absolutely not the right way to build a marriage.

Marriage partners need to provide stability for each other. They need partners upon whom they can rely day by day, and year after year. They need depth of character in their mate; depth that is built upon the stability of God's everlasting Word of Truth.

II Corinthians 2:14:
But the natural man receiveth not the things of the Spirit of God: for they are foolishness unto him: neither can he know them, because they are spiritually discerned.

Don't expect that natural-minded marriage partners will understand the spiritual realties their believing mates value. It will not occur! They lack the spiritual discernment required to do so. They are going to view their believing mate's commitment, to the things of God, to be a waste of time—even foolishness. Talk about disagreement! Talk about discord! Talk about diverse directions! Being yoked in marriage to an unbelieving mate can become like carrying around a heavy dead weight. Here again, God's Word says, DO NOT DO IT! You are going to find enough of a challenge being married to a wonderful believing husband or wife. Do not take on the dead weight of an unbelieving mate. Shared standards and values are absolute requirements to having a peaceful marriage. Be patient, and look to your Heavenly Father—seek His guidance and His blessing in your choice of a marriage partner. Adopt the wisdom of The Word of God as your all-compelling standard. Let it be the victorious standard by which you are going to choose that very, very, special unique individual—with whom you will be yoked together in marriage for the remainder of your days here upon Earth.

It's sure great when our marriage partner has the ability to understand the spiritual realities by which we are surrounded. But, an unbelieving mate lacks this capacity. It needs to be made perfectly clear that unbelievers and God-rejecters are simply not qualified to adequately fulfill the requirements of a godly-ordered marriage. How can they love a wife or a husband with the love of God beaming from their hearts and lives without first loving God? They can not do it because that is impossible.

A good example of a lopsided marriage relationship is the Old Testament record of Nabal and Abigail's marriage.

> *I Samuel 25:3:*
> Now the name of the man was Nabal; and the name of his wife Abigail: and she was a woman of good understanding, and of a beautiful countenance: but the man was churlish [foolish] and evil in his doings; and he was of the house of Caleb.

Nabal is described as being a son of Belial; he worshiped heathen gods. Although he was wealthy, he was also foolish. His sizable herd of sheep grazed safely in a region of Judah controlled by David and his 600 men. David and his men were like a wall around Nabal's herd of sheep, giving them protection as they grazed. At shearing time Nabal rejected David's request for payment for the protection he had provided for his sheep. David refused to accept Nabal's snubbing him. So the disgruntled David mounted his men on horseback and approached Nabal's camp to destroy it. Abigail was a spiritually minded, God-fearing wife. She could see the danger of her husband's foolish decision. She loaded several donkeys with a large provision of food, and quickly travel to meet David to stay-off his anger. It worked! Abigail's godly wisdom prevented David's destruction of Nabal's camp.

> *I Samuel 25: 32-33:*
> And David said to Abigail, Blessed be the Lord God of Israel, which sent thee this day to meet me: And blessed be thy advice, and blessed be thou, which hast kept me this day from coming to shed blood, and from avenging myself with mine own hand.

What a godly woman! The standard by which Abigail lived was the Word of Truth; God's Matchless Word. David could see it; God had sent her to stay off his anger. Her stability was so evident; she listened to her God, and He directed her steps. By hearing God and carrying out what He said to do, Abigail saved her husband's household. She also saved David from avenging himself by the shedding of Nabal's blood.

Nabal's pathway in life led to destruction. He was "without God and without hope." He bowed himself down to worship false gods. He was without the stability of truth. Later, when Abigail told Nabal what had occurred, "his heart died within him, and he became as a stone." Ten days later Nabal died. What a vivid contrast between this foolish God-rejecting husband, and his godly wife. She was in touch with God; but he did not have a clue. Nabal could offer Abigail the wealth of this world, but he could not teach her about the wonderful grace and power of a loving Heavenly Father. His folly was that he had rejected a loving God.

HOW TO GET BORN-AGAIN OF GOD'S SPIRIT

Earlier we touched on the subject of the new birth; however, more needs to be said about this all-important sphere of life. Marriage does not work well in the face of unbelief and God-rejection. Leaving God out of a marriage leads to strife, confusion, and dismay. If a man or woman continues to stumble at the invitation to become born-again of God's spirit they will one-day wander off the deep end of eternity. The unsaved need not remain in their hopeless state. They can respond to the calling of God's love and grace.

God's calling to every individual is to become born-again of His spirit. By believing from the inner recesses of their heart that God raised Jesus Christ from the dead and making Him the living Lord of their life, they will then become born-again and receive holy spirit.

Romans 10:9-10:
That if thou shalt confess with thy mouth the Lord Jesus, and shalt believe in thine heart that God hath raised him from the dead, thou shalt be saved. For

45

with the heart man believeth unto righteousness; and
with the mouth confession is made unto salvation.

The very moment an individual does this, the miracle of all
miracles occurs. God fills them with the gift from above,
holy spirit. The spirit of God in Christ is born in them.
They are no longer just body and soul, now they have spirit
life. They have received the new birth.

Now they have the God-given power that will enable them
to live successfully in this life and in all eternity. They have
the spirit of God in Christ in them. This means that they
now have greater ability than they ever had before! They
are no longer dependent just upon their five senses knowledge. Their capacity has vastly increased. They have the
power of spiritual discernment. Now they can begin to
get serious about the things of God, and the Excellency of
His Word. Now they are able to walk and talk with their
Heavenly Father. His Word has become a light unto their
paths. Now they are empowered with just what they needed
to bring into a marriage union. The potential of a godly
marriage is now a real possibility for them.

A SURE FOUNDATION

Men and women who are born-again of God's spirit have a
rock-solid foundation upon which to build a dynamic life.
Because they are born-again, they are best suited to have
success in the union of marriage. They have the right stuff!
They are armed with ability; the power and presence of

holy spirit resides within them. As they base their marriage decisions upon the Living Word of God, the certainty of what God promises belongs to them. By building upon the standards and precepts of God's Word, and walking in fellowship with Him, their marriage will blossom and abound with blessings. The following hymn, *Heavenly Sunlight*, paints a wonderful picture of the lifestyle born-again husbands and wives can bring to a marriage relationship, day by day. Because they are born-again of God's spirit they serve the same Lord—together they receive His blessings. Their hearts are able to sing in joyous unisons about what they are doing and where they are going together.

> Walking in sunlight, all of my journey; over the mountains, through the deep vale; Jesus has said, "I'll never forsake thee," promise divine that never can fail. Shadows around me, shadows above me, never conceal my Savior and Guide; he is the light, in him is no darkness; ever I'm walking close to his side. In the bright sun light, ever rejoicing, pressing my way to mansions above; singing his praises gladly I'm walking, walking in sunlight, sunlight of love.
>
> *CHORUS*
> Heavenly sunlight, heavenly sunlight, flooding my soul with glory divine: hallelujah, I am rejoicing, singing His praises, Jesus is mine.[4]

As a couple continues to renew their minds to what the Bible teaches about life and marriage, they will excel as husband and wife. Together, they can walk in the heavenly sunlight of God's Word. Together, they can rejoice in God and in one another, while they are pressing their way to mansions above. They are able to enjoy an uplifting life together because, as faithful Believers, they are equipped to carry out God's design for marriage.

CHAPTER 3

TWO FUNDAMENTAL
ELEMENTS OF MARRIAGE

❦

We need to turn our attention to the structure of marriage—how it is put together. We are going to look at two of the essential elements that enable a marriage union to function properly—properly meaning what is required to achieve the purposes God intended. These essential elements are truthfulness and companionship. We will look at the importance of truthfulness first.

TRUTHFULNESS CONFIRMED — VOWING

Maybe there are some that do not fully grasp the significance of making a vow or the taking of an oath. Since getting married involves exchanging vows, let's make sure that we understand the importance of vowing to each other before God. Vows are taken to establish truth and certainty. Usually, God is called upon to witness and ratify the assertions that are promised. It's true that a bride and groom exchange vows to one another at their wedding ceremony; but it is also true, in a Christian ceremony, that God is honored and acknowledged to be a part of the proceedings.

We need to understand the importance God places upon vows. Then we can apply what we have learned to the vows that are made between a man and a woman in a marriage union. Every aspect of vowing a vow to God has great significance—whether in marriage, or any other occasion. God takes vowing before Him seriously, and so must we. Many years ago, I prayed a vow to God concerning a difficulty one of my sons was having in his life. In the vow I promised, "If God would bring about deliverance for my son's problem, I would quit my smoking habit." Well, in less time than a week I bought another pack of smokes and lit one up. As I walked across my front yard, puffing away, God spoke to my mind. He asked, "What is that in your hand?" I immediately dropped the cigarette. God had taken my vow seriously—I had not. God takes our vows to Him seriously enough to hold us responsible for what we say we are going to do. Our relationship with Him must be built upon integrity and truth. We need to back up what we have promised to do, and follow through with the appropriate action.

Now we are going to look at a few scriptures that deal specially with oaths and vows. Because we live in the darkness of a loose moral culture, the validity of an individual's word can fall to the ground quickly. Consequently, the depth of the biblical vow has lost much of its significance in modern day thinking. However, the importance of standing by our word should never be minimized. The first passage we are going to look at cautions the individual, who makes a vow to God, to consider the full ramifications of what he or she has promised to do.

Ecclesiastes 5:4-6:
When thou vowest a vow unto God, defer not to pay it; for he hath no pleasure in fools: pay that which thou hast vowed.
Better is it that thou shouldest not vow, than that thou shouldest vow and not pay. Suffer not thy mouth to cause thy flesh to sin; neither say thou before the angel, that it was an error: wherefore should God be angry at thy voice, and destroy the work of thine hands?

Claiming that a vow was a mistake and lightly dismissing ones' failure to do what was promised to God, or to anyone else for that matter, is definitely fool-hearted. Doing so is a deceitful action that undermines a relationship. This behavior has never been pleasing or acceptable before God. What we need to understand is that He holds us accountable for what comes out of our mouths. (For by thy words thou shalt be justified, and by thy words thou shalt be condemned, Matthew 12:37.) The requirement is that we back up what we have promised to do.

Another helpful scripture we need to consider is in Leviticus. It outlines requirements pertaining to vows or devoted gifts. Under the Levitical Law, every possession that an individual set aside to be given as an offering to the Lord became consecrated. In their Hebrew agrarian setting, individuals would set aside produce, animals, and other gifts they planned to offer up to the Lord later on, at the set time of a feast.

Leviticus 27:28:
Notwithstanding no devoted thing, [what is to be offered to God] that a man shall devote unto the Lord of all that he hath, both of man and beast, and of the field of his possession, shall be sold or redeemed: every devoted thing, [what is to be offered to God] is most holy unto the Lord.

Once a gift was "set aside" to be given to God, it was not to be redeemed or taken back. Every gift set aside or dedicated to God became His alone. Notice also that everything vowed to God was not only holy, it became "most holy." A vow belongs to Him and is not to be esteemed lightly (no reneging). Even though this Old Testament law is not addressed directly to Christian Believers, we can learn and profit from it. I believe every devoted thing (our vow to God) is still "most holy unto the Lord." This is especially true in the marriage covenant.

It is <u>God</u> that joins together a man and a woman in marriage! That which is solemnly vowed between a bride and groom becomes "most holy" before their Heavenly Father. This then is the seriousness of a marriage ceremony. Marriage vows are promises between a man and a woman, but are made before, and unto God. They are essentially the same as a gift unto Him. A marriage covenant is "most holy" in

His sight. God is not just an incidental by-stander who is looking on at a wedding ceremony; He alone is the primary witness. It is not only <u>before</u> Him, it is also <u>by</u> Him, that a bride and groom are bound together in a marriage union— God has joined them together. What is vowed before God is not to be taken back. There can be no justification for light-heartedly claiming that one's marriage was a mistake. When a husband and wife continue to honor their marriage vows, God's abundant blessings can flow upon their lives together.

RASH VOWS

The following Old Testament record from the book of Judges chapter 11 is a good example of a rash vow. Because we can't always see what's ahead in the future, our vows may be more difficult to fulfill than what we imagined. This was true of a man named Jephthah. He led the Israelites into war against the nation of Ammon. As Jephthah marched off to war he made what turned out to be a rash vow. He promised God that he would dedicate to tabernacle service whomever first appeared in the doorway of his home upon returning victoriously over the Ammonites. God gave Jephthah the victory he asked for; however, he was certainly not expecting his only child, a daughter, to be the first to appear at the door upon his return home. Nevertheless, she was the first one he saw. Keeping his promise to God would require giving her up to dedicated service; it was a big decision for him to make. Because Jephthah was a faithful man, he honored what he had promised God he would do. Even though it was very difficult he dedicated his daughter. She agreed with her father's decision and rejoiced with him in the victory that God gave

Israel over the Ammonites. It wasn't an easy thing to do, but Jephthah was a man of integrity, and he honored his word!

Those who are planning to marry need to look long and hard at what may lie ahead. They need to think their potential marriage through as far ahead as possible. Aside from the romance and sexual pleasures that draw a couple into marriage, what comes next? Sometimes it takes years to learn a mate. Dating mostly focuses on the positive assets a couple may share; and very often their love is blinded to the liabilities. A little joke I heard goes like this: Love may be blind, but marriage will open your eyes quickly. How about the family you are marrying into? Do you really know the family your mate comes from; how much time have you shared with them? I have heard it said that, "When you marry a spouse you marry their family also." Take the time to meet them now; get acquainted with them. In the end, you will be glad you did so. If you don't think you can get along with them amiably, now is the right time to find that out.

Have you given due consideration to the positive virtues of honesty and integrity? They are a must. Will this potential mate stick by their word when times get really tough? How about industriousness and thriftiness; how about kindness and thoughtfulness? Is this potential marriage partner a quitter; will they dodge the big issues? Are they prideful? Will they manifest a forgiving heart when they are called upon to do so? Issues like these need <u>serious</u> consideration. Other categories to consider are discipline in the things of God; discipline in business; discipline in temperance. Is this potential mate going to provide the companionship needed for the rest of your days together? Will this man take the God-given responsibility to lovingly care for his mate for the rest of his life? Will this woman submit to her husband and obey what he asks her to do? All of these positive personal traits are a plus for an individual. They are needful just to get along with each other and to enjoy an enduring marriage. This is no time for rash vows! Remember how Jesus encouraged us to "count the cost" of following him as a disciple? We must also "count the cost" of what we are called upon to do in a marriage relationship.

Luke 14:28-30:
For which of you, intending to build a tower, sitteth not down first, and counteth the cost, whether he have sufficient to finish it? Lest haply, after he hath laid the foundation, and is not able to finish it, all that behold it begin to mock him, saying, 'This man began to build, and was not able to finish.'

A COSTLY VOW

A wonderful record of faithfulness to that which was vowed can be seen in the life of an Israelite woman named Hannah. She was barren, and the longing of her heart was to have a son.

I Samuel 1:10-11:
And she was in bitterness of soul, and prayed unto the Lord, and wept sore. And she vowed a vow, and said, O Lord of hosts, if thou wilt indeed look on the affliction of thine handmaid, and remember me,

and not forget thine handmaid, but wilt give unto thine handmaid a man child, then I will give him unto the Lord all the days of his life, and there shall no rasor come upon his head.

God answered Hannah's prayer, and indeed blessed her with a wonderful son. She named him Samuel. The name Samuel means, "because I have asked him of the Lord." Hannah knew, beyond a shadow of a doubt, that this son was a gift from God. She, of course, loved and nurtured Samuel day by day. Finally, the day of his weaning arrived. As tough as it was, still, Hannah dedicates him to tabernacle service for the rest of his days! Without hesitation, she preformed what she had vowed to her Heavenly Father. She made no excuses. She did not bellyache, or find a way to weasel out of what she had promised to do. She joyfully and faithfully honored what she had promised God she would do. Hannah's wonderful heart of thankfulness, and her forthrightness to faithfully give up her son, most assuredly blessed God. In the days that followed, God honored Hannah's faithfulness with the abundant blessing of three additional sons and two daughters.

Vowing in biblical times was voluntary; they were freely spoken. No one was required to make a vow. But once a vow had been established with God, the faithful performance of it became critical. This has not changed, God expects us to honor that which we have promised before Him. The decision to vow a vow in marriage is up to us. It's voluntary; no one has forced us to do so. We choose marriage of our own volition. (Shotgun weddings are mostly in the movies.) It is the faithful performance of our vows that elevates us in the sight of our marriage partner and in the sight of our Heavenly Father. Yes, there will be trying obstacles to overcome—so what, that's life! There will always be tribulation in this world. Christian husbands and wives will need to face difficult days together in the power of the Lord.

To conclude this topic about vows we are going to look at one little section of the parable of the sower. Jesus gave us this parable to teach us how differently people receive the Word of God. We can take his lesson about the seed that fell upon stony places, and make a comparison to a marriage relationship.

> *Matthew 13:20-21:*
> But he that received the seed into stony places, the same is he that heareth the word, and anon [immediately] with joy receiveth it; yet hath he not root in himself, but dureth for a while: for when tribulation or persecution ariseth because of the word, by and by he is offended.

The event of the wedding ceremony is just the beginning of a marriage union. It's a great time of joyous celebration. The outstanding prospects of living life together as husband and wife are very exciting. Nonetheless, it will take "depth of root" to keep a marriage growing and fruitful. Obstacles, temptations, and even tribulations will meet them in the years that lie ahead. Those lacking depth of integrity, and the strength of resolve, will not endure when such trials come; they will be offended. To endure, they will need to cling tenaciously to what they have vowed together before their Heavenly Father. They live in a spiritual arena in this life. It will be the "good ground" of meekness to the Living Word of Truth that will enable their lives together to flourish. By standing upon the Word of God, and remaining faithful to what they promised each other, their marriage will "bring forth fruit, some an hundredfold, some sixtyfold, some thirtyfold. Who hath ears to hear, let him hear" (Matthew 13:8b-9).

A COVENANT OF COMPANIONSHIP

We have seen that a vow establishes truthfulness. Next, we are going to see that a covenant is an agreement between two parties. The terms of the agreement are based upon trust. Because marriage is serious business, God built it upon the cornerstone of a covenant relationship. In a marriage union a man and a woman are bound together in an agreement. They <u>covet</u>, by a vow, to supply companionship to each other for the remainder of their days. Their marriage is to be fostered and strengthened by love. Marriage is a covenant relationship, and is so defined by the Word of God. Because this is true, we need to gain a clearer understanding of what a marriage covenant entails. The verse below refers to "the wife of thy covenant." It is a reference to the covenant union of marriage.

Malachi 2:14:
Yet ye say, Wherefore? Because the Lord hath been witness between thee and the wife of thy youth, against whom thou hast dealt treacherously: yet is she thy companion, and the wife of thy covenant.

Here, in the book of Malachi, God reminds some Judaean husbands that He Himself was a witness to the covenant relationship they entered at the commencement of their marriage. These husbands had become covenant-breakers because they were dealing treacherously (unfaithfully) with their wives by divorcing them. To be confronted by the Lord God of Heaven over the issue of having broken a marriage covenant should have jarred the attention of these men. They absolutely needed to honor what they had sworn before God; this was certainly what God expected them to do. They paid a big price for having broken their marriage commitments; they lost the hand of God's blessings. God even refused to receive their sacrificial offerings. This tremendous record ought to jar our thinking and alert us to the high expectations God puts upon a marriage covenant; He expects husbands and wives to honor their promises. It is plainly clear that a covenant of marriage is highly regarded by God.

So the next thing we are going to do is to look at some covenant records from the Bible. Our goal is not to study all the Bible has to say regarding covenants. Several books could be written on this subject. However, the records we are going to consider will definitely help us to understand important aspects involved in the covenant of marriage. The first covenant recorded in the Bible is one God made with all flesh.

Genesis 9:11-15:
And I will establish my covenant with you, neither shall all flesh be cut off any more by the waters of

a flood; neither shall there any more be a flood to destroy the earth. And God said, This is the token of the covenant which I make between me and you and every living creature that is with you, for perpetual generations: I do set my bow in the cloud, and it shall be for a token of a covenant between me and the earth. And it shall come to pass, when I bring a cloud over the earth, that the bow shall be seen in the cloud: And I will remember my covenant, which is between me and you and every living creature of all flesh; and the waters shall no more become a flood to destroy all flesh.

Notice that this covenant has been established between God and all flesh. Since the days of Noah every human being that has drawn the breath of life has enjoyed the fruits of this covenant. By this covenant, God has established the certainty of His Word. His Word can be trusted. Thousands of years have passed since God made this promise, and He continues to keep it, by faithfulness, day after day. What we need to see here is the certainty of God's Word. This is a major purpose for a covenant. It establishes a declaration of certainty. God has essentially said to us, "This is what I will do, and you can count on it, it is going to come to pass. In all time and eternity nothing can change the certainty of what I have partnered with you by a covenant. My word is steadfast and faithful; openly before all humanity I have proclaimed I will not destroy all flesh from off the face of the earth again by a flood of water." You and I are witnesses to the reality of God's truthfulness. We have seen firsthand that for over 4,000 years God has established the steadfastness of His Word. He has not destroyed all flesh by a flood.

It's easy for us to see how this relates to a marriage covenant. The covenant of marriage establishes a declaration of certainty between a man and a woman. The two of them come together, face-to-face, and essentially proclaim to each other, and before witnesses, "This is what we will do. We agree to provide companionship to one another for the rest of our days upon this earth. You can count on it to come to pass. Nothing is going to take away the certainty of what we have agreed to do. In every situation, under every condition, we agree to honor, to sustain, to love, and to cherish each other. Our words are going to be steadfast and faithful." The certainty of their word will establish their agreement. They have become united by their covenant. It is by the certainty of their words that they have become bound together as husband and wife. The strength of their bond is so strong that they are now "one flesh." The stability of their covenant absolutely rests upon the certainty of their words. There are only two forces that can pry them apart. They can be separated by death, but breaking their word can also tear them apart.

Looking at the Genesis record of the flood, we can see another key aspect of a covenant. God provided a "token of witness." He placed a rainbow in the clouds to serve as a token of the covenant He had established. The rainbow is the testimony, or the witness, of the covenant. When people look up into the clouds and see His rainbow they are reminded of what God promised not to do. The token of a marriage covenant is the wedding ring. The rings that a husband and wife exchange are constant reminders. When they look upon their wedding rings, they can be reminded of what they have promised to each other.

WHO IS LOOKING ON?

Another covenant record that will help us is the one sworn by Jacob and his father in-law, Laban, the Syrian. Perhaps most of us will remember how Jacob ended up working for fourteen years for his wives, Leah and Rachel. Later, when Jacob decided to return to his homeland, without saying a word about leaving to his father-in-law, conflict erupted. The conflict between Jacob and his father-in-law, Laban, was resolved by the making of a covenant. By looking at their covenant agreement, we can learn about the significant role witnesses played. The covenant Jacob and Laban swore was a covenant of separation. They erected a huge pile of stones and agreed that neither one of them would pass by that heap of stones to bring hurt upon the other. In other words, Jacob would not travel past the heap of stones (in a hostile manner) into Syria, and Laban would not travel past the heap of stones (in a hostile manner) into Jacob's home in Canaan. The huge pile of stones they had erected served as a witness to their covenant agreement. Of course, all of the men and women from both camps were witnesses to the covenant proceedings. However, these men called upon a higher witness to sanction their agreement. They called upon the God of Abraham, and Nahor, to witness what they had agreed to do.

Genesis 31:48-54:

And Laban said, This heap is a witness between me and thee this day. Therefore was the name of it called Galeed; And Mizpah; for he said, The Lord watch between me and thee, when we are absent one from another. If thou shalt afflict my daughters, or if thou shalt take other wives beside my daughters, no man is with us; [Here they were in private before God, no man was with them.] see, God is witness betwixt me and thee. And Laban said to Jacob, Behold this heap, and behold this pillar, which I have cast betwixt me and thee: This heap be witness, and this pillar be witness, that I will not pass over this heap to thee, and that thou shalt not pass over this heap and this pillar unto me, for harm. The God of Abraham, and the God of Nahor, the God of their father, judge betwixt us. And Jacob sware by the fear of his father Isaac. Then Jacob offered sacrifice upon the mount, and called his brethren to eat bread: and they did eat bread, and tarried all night in the mount.

Once again, the highest witness present in a marriage ceremony is the God and Father of our Lord Jesus Christ. It is before Him, and unto Him, that a marriage covenant is confirmed. (What therefore "God hath joined together" let not man put asunder, Matthew 19:6b.) God sanctions a marriage pledge of love and faithfulness. He certainly knows what a couple has promised to each other, and what they have sworn to uphold. When couples remain steadfast in what they have promised, the blessings of their Heavenly Father will abound. Couples entering a marriage union must understand that this is a "bond of life and death" they have pledged before God to fulfill. They have obligated themselves both to God and to each other to be "one flesh" for the rest of their days.

GOD'S EXAMPLE SET BEFORE US

We know that God will not deny Himself; He cannot lie. Nonetheless, He has gone beyond the testimony of His written Word and has confirmed it by the oath of a covenant. Because He could swear by no higher, He swore by Himself alone.

> *Hebrews 6:17-18:*
> Wherein God, willing more abundantly to shew unto the heirs of promise the immutability of his counsel, confirmed it by an oath: That by two immutable things, in which it was impossible for God to lie, we might have a strong consolation, who have fled for refuge to lay hold upon the hope set before us.

We have two unchangeable declarations from God—His spoken Word (our Bibles) and the conformation of the immutable covenant He has made with us. The testimony of His covenant being "unchangeable" establishes His written Word. This is a tremendous help for us. Together, these two immutable promises are a "strong consolation." We can rest fully assured that every promise God has made will come to pass.

God has become the pacesetter, so to speak, when it comes to establishing the importance of a covenant relationship. He has entered into a covenant relationship with us. He has obligated Himself to the promises of a new covenant. This new covenant surpasses His covenant not to destroy "all flesh" by a flood of water. By the means of this new covenant God has demonstrated His boundless love.

Matthew 26:27-28:
And he [Jesus Christ] took the cup, and gave thanks, and gave it to them, saying, Drink ye all of it; for this is my blood of the new testament, [new covenant] which is shed for many for the remission of sins.

Hebrews 13:20-21:
Now the God of peace, that brought again from the dead our Lord Jesus, that great shepherd of the sheep, through the blood of the everlasting covenant, Make you perfect in every good work to do his will, working in you that which is well pleasing in his sight, through Jesus Christ; to whom be glory for ever and ever. Amen.

The new covenant God has established gives us the promise of eternal life. We are going to live with Him throughout eternity. The testament of God's sincerity is fully evident. He sealed the covenant that He made with us by the shed blood of His beloved son, Jesus Christ. God has set the standard of covenant making by showing the gravity of His commitment.

Romans 5:8:
But God commendeth [demonstrated] his love
toward us, in that, while we were yet sinners, Christ
died for us.

The depth and integrity of His covenant relationship with
us rest upon His sacrificial giving on our behalf. And, He
has committed Himself to an eternal covenant—it will
never change.

God has set the pattern of what must be practiced in a covenant of marriage between a man and a woman. A husband
and wife must absolutely hear promises that spill forth from
hearts of integrity and resolve. The marriage relationship
they are establishing will require their utmost in sacrificial
giving, and serving. Their wedding vows are locked in place
by an unchanging covenant. These are the qualities that a
man and a woman <u>must</u> bring to the covenant ceremony
of a marriage union—steadfast words of certainty that will
never fall to the ground—immutable words of promise—
words that are salted and will be honored—words of steel
that dispel doubt. The words of a marriage covenant are
the strongest words possible. By the surety of his words,
and her words, they can establish a strong consolation for
each other.

The words of a covenant do not allow abandonment.
In business, contracts are often broken, but marriage
is based on far more than a contract; it is based upon
a covenant that should never be broken—it is 'til death
do us part! It is the decision of a lifetime because it is a

lifetime commitment—there are no, "time outs"—no "I've made a mistake"—no "going back on what you promised to do"—no "the love is gone and my needs are not being met"—no "lighthearted divorces." God does not go back on what He has promised to us. If we are going to be like our Heavenly Father, we must not go back on our word. It's not a lighthearted utterance of " I do" that you are offering in a <u>covenant</u> of marriage. Your words must be ironclad words; staunch weighty words of resolve that endure.

As a couple you may not choose to have the following paragraph read to you as a part of your marriage pledge; however, the two of you need to embrace what it teaches.

> "Your marriage covenant is an 'oath of faithfulness' to which the two of you have committed yourselves; and you have done so in the presence of your Heavenly Father. Your commitment must be considered non-retrievable. This is your word, this is your promise, and it must stand fast for the rest of your days upon this earth. It is your consistent faithfulness to perform that which you have promised that is going to bind you together and establish your marriage. Both of you must honestly accept the full responsibility, the full weight, for what you have promised to faithfully carry out. This is the requirement of what you have lovingly consented to do. What you have solemnly promised to each other can now become the unmovable foundation-rock upon which your marriage can stand."

COMPANIONSHIP

The second fundamental element of marriage we are going to study is companionship. A marriage cannot survive without it.

Genesis 2:18:
And the Lord God said, it is not good that the man should be alone; I will make him an help meet for him.

God designed marriage to do away with the problem of loneliness. The fruits of companionship are the means by which this is achieved. All of us have experienced some degree of loneliness in our lives, and we know firsthand that loneliness "is not good." The union of marriage brings together a man and a woman, who have promised within a covenant, that they will provide companionship to each other for the rest of their days. Companionship equals the sharing of closeness. They are to "cleave" to each other. It is the closeness they share that dispels their loneliness. The fullness of their fellowship binds them together. A husband and wife can share their lives in such a dynamic way that nothing is hid from the other.

Genesis 2:25:
And they were both naked, the man and his wife, and were not ashamed.

Their "nakedness" simply means that Adam and Eve had nothing to hide; nothing was kept back in shame. They enjoyed open acceptance of each other. In the beginning they had no sin; sin entered later. Because they had no sin, they had no shame. Couples today will have sin in their lives; they are two imperfect people. Because this is true, they will need to remain especially honest and open to each other. However, they absolutely must not expect perfection from each other. From time to time, it will be necessary for them to repair the breaches in their marriage that are caused by sins and shortcomings. This is where grace, mercy, understanding, and forgiveness will need to be constantly and tenderly practiced between them.

Adam and Eve shared a mutual responsibility to please God, their Heavenly Father. The first purpose of life is to please God. (When a bride and groom mutually share this tremendous goal they are building their marriage in the Lord.) This will always be a major key to marital success. God made both Adam and Eve; they walked before Him. They talked with Him and He talked with them. He alone had given them life and life together. Companionship for Adam and Eve meant they shared their lives with each other, and also before their Heavenly Father. They lived together, they enjoyed exploring each other's bodies, and they enjoyed sexual fulfillment from each other. They shared togetherness in what they believed. Their purposes in life were the same. Because they had nothing to hide, they enjoyed the fruits of truthfulness and honesty—no lies, no deceptions. They laughed and played together. They worked side-by-side with each other. They built their lives around togetherness. All of this is exactly what companionship means; it's being together and sharing fully.

Companionship is also built upon being together in harmony; having respect, sharing appreciation and love for each other. In companionship aspirations are shared, hopes are shared, longings are shared, bodies are shared, desires are shared, dreams are shared, and purposes are shared. I just can't picture Adam having sent Eve to the far side of the Garden of Eden, so that he could get away from her, can you? No, they needed to be with each other. I believe they worked together in harmony, because they enjoyed the warmth of their loving companionship. Why would he choose a private project that excluded his wife and that took him away from her for days and days on end? Why would she busy herself in pet projects that were more important to her than being a helpmate to her loving husband?

Togetherness defeats loneliness. He goes one way, and she goes the other, will not work in marriage. When her hopes and aspirations are hers, and not his, it will not work. When his dreams and purposes are his, and not hers, it will not work. It is what they can accomplish in sharing and working together that builds companionship. As they labor together in the activities of life, assisting, supporting, and strengthening each other, the bond of their union flowers and blooms. Personally, it's a blessing to have my wife's presence; just to have her in the general vicinity of where I am is pleasing; even comforting. Just to have her near brings joy to my life.

Married couples need to share togetherness mentally, emotionally, physically, and also spiritually. In togetherness they are complete. They have come together in a union that makes them one flesh. Together they have become a husband and wife "glued to each other" for the rest of their days. God helped Adam. He met his need by providing him a wonderful companion. He did not make him a "loner" to live in isolation. The companion God provided was made out of Adam's own flesh. Now that's about as close together as two people can get! This is truly significant. God could have made Eve out of the dust of the earth; that's how He chose to make Adam. Instead, He made Eve out of Adam's flesh. God knew that if Adam was going to lovingly care for anything, he surely was going to lovingly care for someone made out of his own flesh.

Ephesians 5:28-29:
So ought men to love their wives as their own bodies. He that loveth his wife loveth himself. For no man ever yet hated his own flesh; but nourisheth and cherisheth it, even as the Lord the church.

So Adam and his companion, Eve, were made of the same flesh. God brought them together and they became husband and wife; God blessed their union. It is still the same today. A man and his wife are uniquely united in marriage in such a way that the two of them become one flesh. This is the way God designed marriage— two individuals become an entity glued together becoming one flesh. And, the adhesive that binds them together is "loving companionship."

Jay E. Adam's little book, *Marriage, Divorce, and Remarriage In The Bible* is one any couple anticipating marriage would profit by reading. In his chapter, <u>Other Factors,</u> he states:

> The marriage union is the closest, most intimate of all human relationships. Two persons may begin to think, act, feel as one. They are able to so inter-penetrate one another's lives that they become one, a functioning unit. Paul, quoting this verse in Ephesians 5:28-31, says that the relationship is to be so intimate that whatsoever a man does (good or evil) for his wife, he also does for himself since the two have become one flesh (person).[5]

The two of them have become one person in the sense that there is no division between them. Together, they are made whole. She, as his appropriate helpmate in marriage, is his other half. Their union blends them together, making them whole—together they are complete. This is the way they become one flesh, one person. The term "help-mate" in Genesis 2:18 teaches us the <u>purpose</u> a wife is to serve. God designed a wife so that she is able to provide completeness to her other half, her husband. Her beauty, her feminine nature, and her outstanding capacities are meant to enrich his life. He in turn provides his wife with the direction and guidance, protection and provision she needs for her completeness. She enjoys his physical nature and the other masculine characteristics that are uniquely his. Together, they make themselves whole. They are together much more than they could ever be as individuals. The tremendous ways in which they are able to enhance each other is of God's doing; it is of His making. Marriage is His exclusive design and marvelous workmanship.

COMPANIONSHIP DETERRANTS

It's your duty to supply companionship to your mate; this is what you promised to do. It should remain the highest priority of your relationship with each other. Companionship must be cultivated—it takes both time and attention for it to thrive. Whatever gets in the way of companionship is a deterrent to your marriage union. Those things, which destroy our fellowship with God, will also drive a wedge between the hearts and lives of a husband and wife. If an activity were unpleasing to God, why would it please your mate? So, the first key to companionship with your mate is to maintain fellowship with your Heavenly Father. Lies, deception, fears, and negative confessions will never promote unity. Selfishness and egotism breaks the bonds of companionship. Lust, greed, and covetousness undermine all human relationships, including one's marriage relationship. These poor qualities lead to a breach in our fellowship with God and they will certainly destroy companionship with one's spouse.

The necessities of life must be met; food, shelter, clothing—all of these things are required to keep us alive and well. These are fairly simple things to supply in our day because we live in a land of abundance. About 40 hours of labor will do the trick. It is the quest to acquire the bigger house, the bigger bank account, the snazzier car, and the expensive vacation that is going to require a great deal more time and energy. When the acquisition of these things begin to get in the way of marriage companionship they become a deterrent to that marriage. It's kind of like gaining the whole world, but in the process of gaining it you are losing the "soul" of your marriage. The husband that excessively buries his head in business could be burying his marriage also. Spending generous amounts of time together is a must! For a husband and wife to choose a simple lifestyle is a wise decision. The prudent couple will allow no earthly treasures to distract their vision. They will place their "companionship eggs" in the same basket, and they will watch that basket.

The activities we choose to get involved with can be extremely demanding; clubs, sports, fishing, hobbies and pastimes, church duties, committee meetings, and on and on it can go. These demanding activities are usually self-inflicted. If they're getting in the way of fellowship with your mate, they are not worth it; cut back on them or stop them altogether.

Friendship is a great aspect of life; we need our friends. They lift us up and encourage us. They entertain us and they counsel us—what would we do without them? Your spouse should remain your best friend. Other friends cannot be allowed to become an obstacle in your marriage. You have not pledged to provide them with companionship for the rest of your days. Friends and acquaintances do not come before a husband or a wife. A husband and a wife must put each other first before all others. It's great when his friends and her friends are the same friends. From the Christian Believer's point of view, fellowship with the unbelieving and

God-rejecters might be a waste of time unless they become meek to your Christian witness. Some of us have a tendency to witness too much to the goats anyway. What we want to see is the goats move over to the sheep pen.

Serving in the military requires a life dedicated to obeying orders. Your life is certainly not your own in the military. Basically, you go where they tell you to go, and you leave when they tell you to leave. This is a required agenda for the defense of our nation; however, it can be a poor one for the union of marriage. It takes an exceptional couple to withstand the strain and loneliness brought about by long periods of separation. Whenever possible, let the young and unattached, defend us. They will do a great job without the married guys tagging along. If the married guys must serve, good for them; however, they are not exempt from their sworn promise to provide companionship to their marriage partner. The Old Testament law gave a newly married couple exemption from war and also business requirements for the first year of their marriage. God was watching out for a newly married husband and wife. They needed to be together.

Deuteronomy 24:5:
When a man hath taken a new wife, he shall not go out to war, neither shall he be charged with any business: but he shall be free at home one year, and shall cheer up his wife which he hath taken.

War and business are big-time considerations in life. We must defend our nation and it takes a job to keep us fed and clothed. It's plain to see the importance God gives to a married couple being together; it ranks high with Him. What a great way to start a marriage; building depth of companionship and rejoicing in each others company for an entire year, without undue distractions. The priority of companionship will need to stay at the top of the list throughout a married couple's life.

We are told in the Bible that a man shall (is to) leave his father and mother and cleave to his wife (Genesis 2:24). To do otherwise is asking for big-time trouble. There comes a time when a young man and young woman need to step-out on their own; marriage is such an occasion. God knew there could be conflict if a husband and wife chose to live with parents. The goal of parenthood is to rear children so that they are prepared to leave and live independently. The main reason our children need to leave us is that there can only be one head in a home. This is the authority and responsibility that God has placed into the care and keeping of a husband. As the head of that new home, a husband must call the shots. Undue influence and advice from mom and dad are a hindrance; parents need to stay out of the way. A husband and his new wife must establish their own house. They establish the rules and values that they are going to live by. After a couple become husband and wife their first duty is to each other and not to their parents. They may need to lookout for their parents from time-to-time. However, our parent's home is the one they have established, and their home cannot be allowed to over-shadow the home of their offspring. Get far enough away from the shadow of your parents' home that it will not over-shadow your marriage. God has laid before us the proper thing to do in marriage, we are to leave our father and mother's home and cleave to each other, establishing our own home.

Our first duty is to please God. Marriage does not change that reality. What marriage does change however, is that those two individuals have now become one flesh. If a husband is going to love his wife like he loves his own flesh he will not abandon the needs of his wife while he serves in the church. Putting the needs of others before the needs of a mate just won't work! The work of the ministry does not come before the work of companionship in marriage. After the marriage needs are fulfilled, then the needs of the ministry can, and should, be served. We do not serve God in a vacuum; we serve Him through the relationships we share with others, mates are certainly included.

In World War II vast numbers of men were overseas fighting the enemies of the United States. Women were called upon to take up the slack by taking on the work of industry. Their traditional role of "keeper of the home" changed drastically during those days. The advent of the women's liberation movement became another motivator that challenged women to abandon their traditional roles. If the statistics are correct, women make up a little over 50% of the work force today. So today, women embrace careers and pursue them with all endeavor. Her commitment to vocational pursuits is no different than her husband's in regard to not allowing things to get out of bounds. Her vocational pursuits should never overshadow the requirement of companionship that she promised to provide her husband. The couple's unique personalities will determine the need. Some will require more togetherness than others; however, vocational pursuits should never get in the way of the time they need to share with each other. Is her having a job and a career going to be helpful or a hindrance to her husband and her family? The answer to this important question must be answered honestly—if it's a hindrance, don't do it. Too much work makes Jack a dull boy and Jill's over commitment to a vocation can rob her marriage blind. (We will look at other ramifications regarding the wife pursuing a career later.)

There are many other potential deterrents to a married couple's companionship. We cannot cover all of them in this book. It's smart to stay on guard and watch carefully so those deterrent robbers aren't allowed to creep into your marriage. One last comment before we leave this topic concerns the need for personal privacy. It seems that this need varies widely. How much personal privacy (time to be alone) is enough, and how much is excessive: one hour in a day, a day in a week, a week in a month? Just how much do you need and why do you need so much of it? Don't let your prideful ego begin to reign in this matter. Your personal needs, though they may be justified, must blend together with the needs of your spouse. Putting your mate's needs first will help this to balance out for the best. It's just not best to let your personal need for privacy get out of bounds and interfere with the companionship needs of your marriage partner.

CHAPTER 4

HUSBANDS AND THEIR WIVES

❧

THE PROPER ORDER

A wife has every right to expect that her husband will take the position of leadership in their marriage. After all, this is the way God designed the role of a husband to function. A man must take charge; he <u>must</u> take the responsibility for leadership in the marriage if it is to function properly. God placed upon the husband both the authority and the ability of headship. His duty is to lovingly care for his wife and family. He is to provide sound judgments about what they are doing and where they are headed in their lives. It is his responsibility to set the standard by which they must live. The authority of his headship requires that he know about all that is going on in his home and with his family—it is he that must approve issues and decisions because he presides over all.

Today, much of the frustration between a husband and wife is because the husband has failed to rule his wife properly. A husband needs to stand-up and be a man! He needs to be "the man" his wife can count on to lead the way, to set the right standards, and to provide meaningful direction. When he does so, his wife can rest comfortably upon his authority. She needs a husband she can trust to take care of her and their family. A wife will respect a man, all the more, if she can lean on him and the stability he is to provide. "The buck stops here," as President Truman said years ago in reference to his office of the presidency. The authority of the husband requires that "the buck stops here" with him, who is the head of his wife and children— and yes, he is to be a very loving authority. The rule of love is the means by which he is to practice his position of authority. Whenever the husband falters or abdicates his position of authority, big time problems will follow.

The proper "godly arrangement" of marriage is outlined for us by the following:

I Corinthians 11:3:
But I would have you know, that the head of every man is Christ; and the head of the woman is the man; and the head of Christ is God.

God expects us to acknowledge that He is over all. He is the Creator, the Ruler and Sustainer of Life. Jesus Christ, God's only begotten son, always submitted to his Father. He did so faithfully throughout his lifetime here on earth; "not my will but thine be done," was his prayer in the

Garden of Gethsemane just before he obediently gave up his life on the cross. The husband is to submit to the headship of Jesus Christ. He is to submit to the headship of Christ after the same fashion that Christ submitted to his Heavenly Father. The wife is to submit to her husband in the same manner her husband submits to his head, Jesus Christ. This is the arrangement God established and it works best! No other arrangement works better. **This is the heart and guts of how we are to relate to each other in marriage**.

Once again, God placed the responsibility of authority upon the shoulders of the husband and not on the wife— her responsibility is to obey her husband. To veer away from this godly order and set up an apostate standard will not work. It's doomed to failure! This is one major reason why marriages break apart and fail. One, or perhaps both partners are out of sink with the required order God established. Within this "proper order" the husband submits to his head; to a loving Jesus Christ, and the wife submits to her loving husband—if he is doing his job the right way he is a loving husband.

LOVE CONSTRAINS

When did Jesus Christ ever force anyone to obey his will? Biblically, submission is to always work within the bounds and framework of love. (Later we will study biblical submission in more depth.) Marriage is a vital love relationship. Depth of love is the fuel that keeps it travelling along successfully. Submitting is not to be some kind of enormous pill to swallow; it's not to be a high mountain to climb; rather, it is obedience to the high calling of a love relationship. Normally, obedience is a natural response to love bestowed upon a wife by her husband. (We will deal with the oddballs later.) It is certainly the love that God has for us that moves us to obey Him. He woos us with His goodness. It is the depth of the love of Jesus Christ, that he would lay down his life, which constrains us to love him in return.

> *II Corinthians 5:14-15:*
> For the love of Christ constrains us; because we thus judge, that if one died for all, then were all dead:
> And that he died for all, that they which live should not henceforth live unto themselves, but unto him which died for them, and rose again.

It's the depth of a husband's love for his wife that constrains her. His love woos her positive response of obedience. As a beautiful wife learns to obey her husband, her life will become joyous. As she lovingly submits to her husband she is behaving within the framework of her Heavenly Father's will. This is the way God designed her to function. Her life is then freed up from cares and responsibilities that are better left to her husband. She will not be "twisted out of shape" by responsibilities that belong to him. A Christian wife needs to maintain a trusting, positive, attitude toward what God has asked her to do. The trust and confidence she has in God's marriage plan will put her wonderful heart at ease. She also needs to maintain a peaceful, trusting, attitude about her husband's ability to make sound judgments for their lives. He needs for her to confidently support him in every way. And yes, he will be mistaken in his decisions, from time to time.

LOVE'S RESPONSE

The wife's support of her husband is like the strong timbers that are needed to build a house.

Proverbs 14:1:
Every wise woman builds her house, but the foolish plucketh it down with her hands.

By "backing-up" her husband she is building the framework of their marriage; she's fortifying their union. In doing this she will also bring gratification and satisfaction to her own life. She's accomplishing something of great importance. She is fulfilling her God-given purpose! Supporting her husband's leadership will bring fulfillment to her life. She is to share in the glory of her husband's victories. They are not just his victories, they are "their" victories. The help and support she brings to the life of her husband has helped to produce those victories. They glory together because they're on the same team. It is her tremendous help that enables his success. A good example of this can be found in the description of a virtuous woman from the book of Proverbs.

Proverbs 31:23:
Her husband is known in the gates, when he sitteth among the elders of the land.

Here is the result that can come to pass by the helping hand of a supportive wife. The verse above describes how a woman's husband has risen to a place of prominence in the government of their city. This wife's dedication and support helped her husband to ascend to his lofty position in their community. Whenever a wonderful wife is both a helper and companion she brings encouragement into their marriage. On a personal note, my wife, Carol, has been a helpmate to me throughout the 34 years of our marriage. She has been happy and gratified to do so. Her support has encouraged my life. I am so much more because of her helping hand. Her help and support inspires me to be my best. What a woman! What a wife! I am so blessed by her giving heart.

IT TAKES TWO TO TANGO

I Corinthians 11:8,9,11:
For the man is not [made] of the woman; but the woman of the man. Neither was the man created for the woman; but the woman for the man.
Nevertheless, neither is the man without the woman, neither the woman without the man, in the Lord.

God designed the role of the husband into the very structure of marriage. Adam was not created originally for the sake of Eve. The opposite is true, a woman was created for the sake of a man. God did not make a man out of a woman. He did not ask a man to submit to his wife. He did not ask a wife to be the head of her husband. All of this would be contrary to the way God designed life and marriage to function. As far back as the Garden of Eden, God placed the role of leadership squarely upon the shoulders of the husband.

Genesis 3:16:
Unto the woman he said, I will greatly multiply thy sorrow [labor] and thy conception; in sorrow [labor] thou shalt bring forth children; and thy desire shall be to thy husband, and he shall rule over thee.

Maybe the awesome responsibility of birthing a child requires much more than we men ever think about. We need to give it its due consideration. My wife shared some of the following about birthing a child:

- A woman's body goes through tremendous changes.
- She has to guard her diet.
- She has to deal with carrying extra weight around.
- Changes come upon her and she becomes subject to them.
- Her emotions are much more sensitive.
- Nine months gets to be so long, and it really takes a great deal of patience to endure.
- When the contractions start, it's like they are cast upon her, and she cannot control them, they control her.

"Labor" is the right word because it takes all the stamina and strength she can muster to push her baby from her abdomen through her dilated vagina, and finally out of her body and into the world. This is her work, this is her job, and this is also her joy and responsibility. She was created with this glorious capacity!

A man is by her and not of himself. It is she that brings forth the birth of a child. Adam is the only man not born of a woman, the rest of us were. It is because of her that a birth can come to pass—"neither is the man without the woman." A man is totally dependent upon his wife to birth their children, and without her willingness to do so there will be no offspring—she alone has the ability to birth a child. Her physique, her temperament, her emotional makeup, her motherly capacity, these are all of God's design—God built her just that way. Because of all these tremendous characteristics, she is also best suited to care for a child. The work of nurturing a child is the work of a mother. The father is to lovingly watch over them.

A wife is to lovingly submit to the authority of her husband. And, let it be said emphatically, she will not do so by constraints, by demands, by threats, by harassing and forcing; but she can do so with a willing heart in response to a loving husband. The position of a husband, to be the "head of the woman," is not a glorified status; it's not a "higher position" of glory than that of his wife. Nor is it a lowly, demeaning, position for a woman to submit to her husband. Rather, this is the natural order that is best suited for both the woman and the man—this is exactly the way they are designed to function. Author, Debi Pearl, says the following about her relationship with her husband.

> My husband does not lose any dignity by being in subjection to Christ, nor do I lose any dignity by being in subjection to my husband. And, just as my husband finds security and meaning in submission to his head, so I become the person God created me to be in submitting to my head—my husband.[6]

A husband and wife certainly need each other. They should never squabble over leadership responsibilities. They are made to compliment one another as they function in their God-given roles. In togetherness, they make each other complete!

There is considerable tension between husbands and wives in our modern society. A great deal of this contention emanates from a failure to understand proper God-given marriage roles. The television entertainment industry contributes to this failure by constantly undermining marriage roles. They generally portray the husband to be a dummy. They show him to be incapable of leadership. He's made to look like a dunce. They show the wife to be the one "in the know"—she rules the roost. Her husband basically does what she tells him to do, and that's the end of it. He's a "hen-pecked" man, and when she says jump, he jumps. It's sad to say, but in many cases there is some justification for these disturbing portrayals. For marriage to work properly a husband needs to accept his God-given responsibility to be the loving head of his wife, and his wife needs to lovingly obey God and submit to her husband. Couples who do otherwise, and embrace twisted, worldly, ideas about marriage are in big-time trouble. The contention and frustration they are experiencing will continue until they harmonize their behavior so that it lines up with the accuracy of what God's Word proclaims.

WHOSE HEAD IS COVERED?

In the book of First Corinthians chapter 11, we're going to look at a few verses that deal with a marriage custom practiced in the early Christian church. These verses will help us to see a little about how husbands and wives behaved themselves toward one another, and especially in their public church fellowships.

> *I Corinthians 11: 4:*
> Every man praying or prophesying, having his head covered, dishonoureth his head.

In a Christian Fellowship of the first century, if a man were to show up with a shawl covering his head he would have become a laughingstock. He never would have done such a thing. A shawl on his head would have signaled, to everyone present, that he was under the authority of his wife—that she was the head of the family. It would have signaled that his wife was calling the shots; she was in control of things. Such a man would have been tremendously shamed and disgraced before the church. He would have brought dishonor to himself.

Today, we do not see husbands wearing shawls on their heads. But if they were truthful concerning what is actually occurring in their marriage relationships, you would see a tremendous number of husbands wearing shawls. Actually, it's just as shameful today as in the first century to see a man "whimping" around and allowing his wife to run their marriage because he has failed to take charge. He dishonors himself when he allows his wife to be the head in their home. It is absolutely ridiculous to see a man shirk his responsibility and allow his wife to dominate their union. In many instances she feels the need to take up the slack because her man is not living up to his job. This kind of marriage behavior is unbecoming to both of them. They are both out-of-step with how their marriage roles should function. Maybe husbands today should be truthful enough to wear shawls on their heads, or else take charge in their marriages. The paramount need is that they take charge! Their wives will respect and praise them for having done so.

I Corinthians 11:5:
But every woman that prayeth or prophesieth with her head uncovered dishonoureth her head: for that is even all one as if she were shaven.

A tradition the First Century Church practiced called for a woman's head to be covered in a public fellowship. The shawl she wore on her head represented the covering her husband's life provided for her. He was her protector and provider, and she depended upon his lordship. Wearing her shawl was the outward sign that she reverenced her husband's position of authority by submitting to him. If a married woman were to show up with her head uncovered, others would feel she was behaving in an unbecoming fashion. The outward sign of a prostitute, in those days, was a shaven head or cropped hair. For a married woman to show up with no covering on her head was, in the eyes of their fellowship, comparable to the behavior of a prostitute. My thinking is that even if she did not respect her husband in her heart, she still showed up with the shawl on her head. The important thing for us to see here is that the standard set in the First Century Church was that a wife was <u>expected</u> to honor and obey her husband. However, this is not the normal thing we are seeing in our day. You know it, and I know it! This needs to change. For marriage to work, husbands and wives absolutely need to get with the program that's outlined for them in the Living Word of God; it is here they will learn how to behave properly towards one another.

ONE FLESH

After a man and woman are pronounced husband and wife, life changes for them. Now they have a brand-spanking new look. They are no longer just two individuals trying to get along with their own private concerns. They still have individual bodies; however, they have agreed to bind themselves together in great unity. They have agreed upon the same aspirations, the same expectations, the same desires, and the same commitments to each other. Now, they even share the same name. God has joined them together so that they are no longer two isolated individuals. They have become uniquely bound together as one flesh. God Himself refers to them as "one flesh." The term "one flesh" may be considered figurative in the view that a husband and wife still retain their two unique bodies. However, a husband and wife are one flesh literally in the sense of their commitment to unity of love and lifetime faithfulness to each other. The bond of two hearts can be so strong that it literally binds individuals together in unions that are unbreakable except by death. This is to be the strength and depth of love that draws a man and a woman together in the unity of marriage. Obviously, their two bodies do become one in sexual intercourse, but it is the depth of their love that keeps them continuously united.

Ephesians 5:28-29:
So ought men to love their wives as their own bodies. He that loveth his wife loveth himself. For no man ever yet hated his own flesh; but nourisheth and cherisheth it, even as the Lord the church.

A husband has become joined with a wife whom he must treat just like his own flesh if his marriage is going to flourish and endure. So how does a man treat his own flesh? The answer to this is so obvious; he nourishes it—he sustains it with all that is necessary to life and growth. He cherishes it. He values his body highly—he gives it tender loving care. He wants the best for that body of his. He grooms it even to the point of perfection. So how does a man treat the wife of his own flesh? He treats her in the same way; he tenderly nourishes and cherishes her. He wants to provide the very best for her. How can a man be a good husband and treat his wife with less care and love than he treats himself?

The high calling of a Christian marriage sets forth a standard, which asks a man to "love his wife even as Christ also loved the church."

Ephesians 5:25-27:
Husbands, love your wives, even as Christ also loved the church, and gave himself for it. That he might sanctify and cleanse it with the washing of water by the word, That he might present it to himself a glorious church, not having spot or wrinkle or any such thing: but that it should be holy and without blemish.

At this point, we need to stop and think about what Jesus Christ's love accomplished for the church. Oh, the price he paid to make us whole! His boundless love paid the price to cleanse us from all our sins. Because of his love, and giving, men and women can become born-again of God's spirit. He has brought us newness of life. To accomplish all of this it required that he lay down his life. This is, of course, the greatest love a man can have—that he would lay down his life for his friends (John 15:13). What a tremendous example! This is so big! A husband is admonished to love after this pattern.

I doubt that any of us are going to match the love Jesus Christ has for the Church—he never blundered one time. However, the glowing, elevated, example of his love is set before us—and how glorious it is! Now a husband can measure the quality of the love he has for his wife by this great standard. Some of the following are going to be required to achieve it—it's going to take a good supply of patience and a determined, willful, disciplined effort. It will take understanding and forbearance. For husbands to love their wives with Christ-like selfless giving will require a spir-itually-minded walk. They will certainly need to shed some of their "old-man" habits and renew their minds to the high standard of what God asks husbands to do. Well men, it's a lot to live up to! But, what are we going to do—choose a lesser standard? A lesser standard than that of the love of Jesus Christ will just not work. And yes, this is the kind and quality of love any wife will joyously receive. This is the mortar that will build beauty and strength in a marriage.

The accomplishments brought about by the love of our Lord Jesus Christ are breath- taking. It's no wonder God has highly exalted him, and has given him a name above every name. When a husband follows after this same example of Christ-like loving, his marital works are going to accomplish some tremendous things. He will become a buckler and shield for his wife. He will provide watchful care over her. He'll shelter and protect her life from devil-ish doctrines and the cunning craftiness of men and any other threats to her well being. He will provide for her in the best possible fashion he can muster by the labor of his hands, and the sweat of his brow. He'll provide spiritual leadership to his wife and their children by the example of his faithful living before God—he'll be a sure and steadfast spiritual guide for their lives. His wife can depend upon the soundness of his decision-making because he stands rock-solid upon God's Word of Truth. These are some of the uplifting qualities a wife needs in her man. And when she gets them her life will be comforted, encouraged, inspired, and joyfully fulfilled.

THE LOVE OF GOD

God Himself has taught us how to love. He demonstrated His love for us in that while we were yet sinners, without strength, He gave us life through the sacrificial death of His only begotten son (Romans 5:8). And now this "love of God" is in us by virtue of the fact that we are born-again of His spirit. God has given us of His spirit! What a glorious work! His abiding presence within us proves His love. And, because we are sons of God, we have been given the capacity to manifest His love. Yes, we have the ability to love with the love of God! However, this love will remain dormant until we bring it out into the open. We must, by our conscious decision and deliberate action, practice loving like this—giving, serving, blessing, and praising. This is the way God's love is going to be seen in us. We bring it out into the open by the way we live. We practice it by putting it into action. The measure of our spiritual maturity is the extent to which we have learned to operate the love of God in our lives. This is the thing that counts the most about our Christian witness. Our actions are the proof of our love. How religious we are is not the standard. Feeding the poor is not the standard. Even the glory of giving one's body to be burned is not the right standard. Jesus said it so plainly:

John 13:35:
By this shall all men know that ye are my disciples, if ye have love one to another.

Charitable love is the love of God actively at work in the heart of a believing Christian. Getting this love of God into our marriage is what we must do. The manifestation of charity between a man and his wife is the pathway to a happy marriage union. The Bible is clear concerning the fabric of what charitable love is. The reference below is a good description of charitable love.

> *I Corinthians 13: 4-7: (The Amplified Bible)*
> Love endures long and is patient and kind; love never is envious nor boils over with jealousy, is not boastful or vainglorious, does not display itself haughtily. It is not conceited (arrogant and inflated with pride); it is not rude (unmannerly) and does not act unbecomingly. Love (God's love in us) does not insist on its own rights or its own way, for it is not self-seeking; it is not touchy or fretful or resentful; it takes no account of the evil done to it [it pays no attention to a suffered wrong].
> It does not rejoice at injustice and unrighteousness, but rejoices when right and truth prevail. Love bears up under anything and everything that comes, is ever ready to believe the best of every person, its hopes are fadeless under all circumstances, and it endures everything [without weakening].[7]

What a wonderful challenge! We can work on loving in this manner day-by-day for the rest of our days. This is the dynamic way we are "called to love" as husbands. What a standard! This is the depth of love we must learn to show forth to our wives; yes, to love them with the love of God that is alive within us. God has defined the role of a husband;

and, this is it! This is the way God intends for a husband to love his wife.

TURN YOUR GENERATOR ON

The Bible does not teach, "Wives, love your husbands even as Christ loved the church." It teaches that husbands are to do that. It's obvious that God expects the husband to generate love in his marriage. So we men need to turn our generators on. We are the ones who are to generate love toward our wives. We certainly have the capacity to do so. One great thing about our wives, men, is that they are like highly polished mirrors. They reflect very well. Under normal circumstances, our wives are going to reflect the love we give to them. The love they receive from us will literally bounce right back to us. And, if there is a cripple-hearted wife that does not respond in this manner, so what! What better thing would motivate her? Nothing would! So we just keep on loving and giving. Love can heal even a crippled, closed-off, heart.

> *I Corinthians 11:7: (Phillips translation)*
> A man ought not to cover his head, for he represents the very person and glory of God, while the woman reflects the person and glory of the man.

We have already discussed the covered head aspect of this verse. What we need to discover now is that a husband is to represent the glory of God to his wife. He does this by the way he shows godly characteristics in his life; kindness, mercy, love, generosity, forgiveness, grace, and so forth—his life is a reflection of God's goodness. God's goodness is alive within that husband and he shows forth that goodness to those around him and especially to his wife. Jesus said, "He that hath seen me hath seen the Father" (John 14:9). Wouldn't it be great if our wives could say of us, "When I see my husband, he reminds me of my Heavenly Father."? This is the way it can and should be! In like manner, when a wonderful wife looks upon her husband and sees his godliness and generosity she will be inclined to reflect these same qualities. The natural thing for her is to respond in kind. What she has received from her husband, that which he has shown forth to her, she will naturally reflect in her life. This is how beautifully it works. It's a big winner for both the husband and the wife. This is the way God set it up. This is the way a husband represents the very person of God to his wife, and this is the way a wife reflects the person of her husband. This is the godly way marriage is designed. Marriage is truly the handiwork of our Heavenly Father!

By the way, she may be physically weaker than her husband, but she will not be forced beyond her willingness. When a husband treats his wife poorly; ignores her and berates her; downs her; speaks harshly to her; she is going to reflect this treatment back to him as well. Remember, God "first loved us," and now we love Him in return (I John 4:19). The need is that we sow the good seed of kindness, generosity, respect, admiration, consideration, and charity into the good ground of our marriage. In the end, we are going to reap from that woman of ours, a bountiful supply of just what we need. When a wife understands that she occupies first place in the heart of her husband, she is indeed a "happy camper."

A HUSBAND'S RESPONSIBLITY

Genesis 2:21-22:
And the Lord God caused a deep sleep to fall upon Adam, and he slept: and he took one of his ribs, and closed up the flesh instead, thereof; And the rib, which the Lord God had taken from man, made he a woman, and brought her unto the man.

God constructed the woman out of the man's flesh, and "brought her" to Adam. God gave her to him! She became His gift to Adam. Adam then became responsible for Eve. Whenever we receive a gift we become responsible for it because it now belongs to us. In his small book, *Light Through An Eastern Window*, Bishop K.C. Pillai describes one aspect of an Eastern marriage ceremony.

There is no wedding ring as there is in the Western world. Instead, a silver cord is placed around the girl's neck. The groom may now lift the veil and view for the first time the wife whom he has married, having never known her before.

He slowly raises the veil with fear and trembling and places it upon his shoulder. This symbolizes that the girl's God-given protection is now on his shoulder. Her care and protection are now his responsibility and he is therefore as God to her. This is the meaning of the phrase in Isaiah 9:6, "and the government shall be upon his shoulder." Christ bought us for a price, and as our bridegroom he has taken the responsibility for us on his shoulder.[8]

This same principle is true in a Western marriage. You, the husband, must take upon your shoulders the responsibility for the woman you are marrying. You become responsible before God for her care and well being. She's God's gift, but now she belongs to you. Don't be surprised to see her looking up to you very much like you must look up to your Heavenly Father. She is going to be looking to you for her security and well being. She will need for you to provide a dwelling place, food, and clothing. She will expect that you provide for her comfort and her pleasure. She will also expect you to be a guide and an inspiration for her life. These are some of the things that she will expect of you, her husband. You have become the man to whom she now must submit. She is obligated before God to do so. Now it is both your privilege and your duty to care for her; to enjoy her; to be her guide and stay; to sustain and protect her; to provide for her and to love and cherish her for the rest of your days together.

ESTABLISHING DECISIONS

We need to briefly study a section of scripture from Numbers chapter 30. It will teach us some of the depth of how a husband and his wife are to function in marriage. Here we are going to see how a husband bears the responsibility to care for his wife's best interest, her welfare, and her wholeness. As we saw earlier, under the requirement

of the Old Testament law, every vow made before God must
be honored.

Numbers 30: 2:
If a man vow a vow unto the Lord, or swear an oath
to bind his soul with a bond; he shall not break his
word, he shall do according to all that proceedeth
out of his mouth.

This was true for both men and women. "Every" vow or
oath made by a husband, or a wife, unto God must be honored. This is what God required. However, there was an
exception in the case of a married woman's having made
a vow. She needed her husband's approval for her vow to
stand.

Numbers 30:13-16:
Every vow, and every binding oath to afflict the soul,
her husband may establish it, or her husband may
make it void. But if her husband altogether hold his
peace at her from day to day; then he establisheth
all her vows, or all her bonds, which are upon her:
he confirmeth them, because he held his peace at
her in the day that he heard them. But if he shall
any ways [at a later time] make them void after that
he hath heard them; then he shall bear her iniquity.
These are the statutes, which the Lord commanded
Moses, between a man and his wife, between the
father and his daughter, being yet in her youth in
her father's house.

A wife enjoyed the freedom to make vows. However, if she had made a rash vow, by not first conferring with her husband, God placed the duty of establishing the vow she had made upon her husband. The very day her husband learned of the vow she had made his responsibility was to allow it, if he thought it was the right thing for her to do, or to void it if he thought it was out-of-step with her well being. His silence in this matter was the same as a confirmation. In other words, if he said nothing the vow was established before God. If the husband, on a later occasion, changed his mind and negated her vow, his wife was to obey his decision, but the husband, himself, would pay the penalty for breaking the vow he had established earlier.

That the Lord God of Heaven and Earth would allow a husband to actually invalidate a vow his wife had sworn unto Him ought to speak loudly to everyone. It certainly emphasizes the important significance of a husband's decision-making authority. The responsibility he bears requires that he provide guidance and direction for his spouse. From God's point of view He expects a husband to confirm or void even the heartfelt religious devotions of his wife; not by constraint or from a selfish, self-seeking, motive, but because her well being is in his hands. His loving guidance should be a wall of protection around her life. A loving husband will want the very best for his wife. His help can, and should, be a guiding light that gives direction for their lives together.

Unity of purpose between a husband and his wife is essential to their well being. If she is going in her own self-chosen direction and he chooses another, their marriage is on a bumpy road. The husband's role is to be the guiding head. He alone must provide leadership for their union. If he is a godly husband he will be looking to his head—the Lord Jesus Christ. God's expectation is that the husband takes the full responsibility for directing his marriage. The husband, alone, must establish the direction of their activities and their commitments. His duty is to get involved with the heart-felt needs of his wife and take care of those needs. He is not to be "sidetracked" or consumed by any greater interest than his wife and their family.

LEADERSHIP MANAGEMENT

The husband is the head of his household and he needs to manage it well. First, he must manage himself well because he is responsible for all that goes on within his family. Isn't it interesting to see how a qualification for leadership, as an elder in the church, requires that a man rule his own house well?

> *I Timothy 3:4-5:*
> One that ruleth well his own house, having his children in subjection withall gravity; (For if a man know not how to rule his own house, how shall he take care of the church of God?)

The elder was to be an example to his flock. He must rule his house well. This is what a husband must do also. His job is to preside over his wife and children and give direction for their lives. In other words, he guides their abilities by providing them the direction they need. As a good manager he must delegate responsibilities to his family. The wife is in charge of the responsibilities that have been delegated to her. Here, her power of decision making is essential. A good manager would never put his thumb on anyone's personality. He is not to become a dictator. The management of his family requires tender, loving, thoughtful, care. Love is the power that persuades! He will need to look well to the state of their activities, and stay abreast of what they are involved with—his family must answer to him and to his guidance. Their needs must be served even before his own. It is his job to see that their needs are met on a regular basis because needs are going to be constantly changing.

All of this comes under the job description of a husband. He's the head that provides direction for his family and food for their table; he's their shoulder to cry on; he's their helping hand; he's their understanding counselor, and he's their wise advisor. A Christian husband is a man of God whose heart is lovingly set upon caring for the needs of his wife and family. His authority as the head of their home should never become an offence to his wife because he is to be a buckler and shield for her. She can glory in the warmth of his goodness, his tender loving care, his thoughtful giving hand, and the bountiful supply of his labor. He's not only "her man," he is first and foremost "God's man" The stability of his spiritual strength will be a restful, inspiring, place for his wife to abide. She is tucked-in securely under his loving, protective, wing.

To repeat what was said before, loving our wives after the pattern of Christ's love is going to require a great deal of conscious effort. It will not just occur out of the blue. We will need to strive with purpose-of-heart to do so. She might not always be so appealing and loveable; at times she might be distant and moody, even angry and critical. How are we going to handle contentions that may arise between us? Contentions and strife will undermine the pleasant atmosphere of the home and destroy the peacefulness of any relationship.

Proverbs 21:9: (The Amplified Bible)
It is better to dwell in a corner of the housetop (on the flat oriental roof, exposed to all kinds of weather) than in a house shared with a nagging, quarrelsome, and faultfinding woman.[9]

No one would choose to marry a nagging, quarrelsome, faultfinding, woman. It is those who become this way, later on in the marriage, that's the problem. If you have found a sinless woman for your mate, one whose mind is perfectly renewed to the Word of God, "good" for you! (Live with her a little longer and then tell us this is still true.) The truth of the matter is, she will need room for growth because her mind is not perfectly renewed to the Word of God. The reality of your marriage is going to prove, that just like you, she will not always get it right. She is going to need your forgiveness and kind-hearted understanding, from time to time, just as you will need hers.

Settling issues, and forgiving sins and mistakes, is a part of the marriage turf—even the best of marriages will require this. In critical times of contention between the two of you, you, the husband, will need to step forward and demonstrate your special brand of tender- loving leadership. Remember, first of all, everything that you are required to do for a sister-in-Christ you must quickly do for your wife. Your being the "good example" may require gut-level determination; nonetheless, be daring enough and do it—doing so will encourage an environment of reconciliation. If you're a man of spiritual depth and perception, what a plus that will be for the two of you! Remember that it was when we were without hope and marred in sin that God thought enough about us to give us newness of life. A husband's gracious love, mercy, and forgiveness, in hard desperate times of contention, is like a healing balm, it can heal even the deepest of wounds.

DIRECTIVES FOR WISE HUSBANDS

What is the quality of life you are going to live before your wife? Your living standards should never be based upon the worldly values of natural-minded men. She already knows about your positive assets, your morality, and your appeal. But, your standard of values must rest solidly upon a sure and lasting foundation. In the Bible there is an abundance of specific instructions that are designed to teach husbands exactly what they need to understand about themselves and their wives. (Very valuable marital information, I must say!) I have entitled this section <u>Directives For Wise Husbands</u>. We do not have the space here to fathom-out all of these powerful directives. However, it will pay big dividends if you follow through and search them out and apply them—this is what you need to do. We are going to take the time to look at some of them:

> *I Peter 3:7:*
> Likewise, ye husbands, dwell with them, according to knowledge, giving honor unto the wife, as unto the weaker vessel, and as being heirs together of the grace of life; that your prayers be not hindered.

If we husbands are going to dwell with our wives according to knowledge, then we <u>must</u> become ardent students of God's Word. Here, we will find the knowledge that will enable us to "get it right" in our marriages. Here, all things that pertain to "life and godliness" are spelled-out plainly for us—precepts upon precepts, statutes upon statutes, testimonies upon testimonies, and judgments upon judgments. We absolutely need to study to show ourselves approved unto God—how else are we going to learn His will? As we study and learn, we will then understand how to dwell joyously with our wives. No matter what the situation may require of us, we will be ready—we can apply the understanding we have gained from *The True Source Book of Marriage* (The Bible). We will have chosen to confidently lean upon the ever-lasting Word of the Lord. This then is a very large aspect of how we dwell with our wives "according to knowledge."

There are still other considerations when it comes to dealing with our wives "according to knowledge." We should leave no stone unturned in our effort to understand them, and to be a blessing to them. Obviously, the authority of a husband is not to over-ride the personality of his wife. She must choose, by the freedom of her will, to lovingly respond to her man. A husband provides direction for his wife but a wife needs adequate space to exercise her abilities and talents. She will get the job done, don't "horn-in" and hinder her efforts. No husband should undermine his wife's talents. A woman's gift "maketh room" for her just like a man's does. Indeed, if she is a wise woman she will continue to build her house. A husband's decision-making must take into account his wife's valuable input. He should listen with a careful ear and reap the benefit of her helpful perspective. Her feminine nature, quite often, views circumstance in ways that are unique to her gender. What a waste it would be to neglect what she has to offer. The wise husband will not only allow his wife's opinion, he will encourage her to make full use of her talents and abilities. As long as her heart is to bless her husband, and household, her strengths are going to be a big plus for the entire family.

Proverbs 31:26-27:
She openeth her mouth with wisdom; and in her tongue is the law of kindness. She looketh well to the ways of her household, and eateth not the bread of idleness.

God can, and does, speak to the heart and life of a Christian wife. From time to time, she may receive just the right information that's needed concerning a given situation. As she remains a meek servant of our Lord Jesus, and abides within her God-given framework of submission to her husband, she is a glory to her Savior. Her love for God, and knowledge of His Word, truly elevates the value of what she has to say. Her intelligence is a plus, her wisdom and understanding is a plus, her spiritual insight becomes a plus—all that God has placed within her wonderful life can be, and should become, an outstanding blessing to her husband and others. The "law of kindness" that is in her tongue can direct her speech—it won't allow for critical, cutting, negative, words. Her uplifting words of grace and favor are going to be like the spice-of-life to the ears of her spouse. The healing, helpful, words that are coming from her lips will bring refreshing joy to the lives of her entire family.

When it comes to decision-making authority in a marriage, a wife must not insist that her opinion prevail. The husband alone is responsible before God to lead the way, to be the decision-maker. Because this is true, a wife's opinion must be offered in a spirit of meekness, and generosity, that honors her husband's position. Her submission and meekness to him is a duty before God. If a wife demands that her decisions must prevail and her husband gives into her, they both are missing the mark. This kind of behavior is completely "out-of-step" with the order God established for marriage. What is practiced today, when the wife becomes the head of her husband, is a worldly standard that generally leads to misery for both of them.

In I Peter 3:7, we are taught that physically the wife is a weaker vessel. So, the husband needs to take note of this and be careful with her. He certainly needs to remain sensitive about his wife's strength and stamina. He simply is not to put more on her than she can physically perform. She is not to be overtaxed with a physical workload too hard for her to handle. Nor is she to be overtaxed with more responsibility than she can comfortably handle in any other category. Too much responsibility can cause a lot of wrinkles on a lovely face. She should not be overtaxed with undue responsibilities that distract from her ability to care for her children and her home. They should remain her highest calling. Someone must care for the children and the home. Who can do it better than a loving wife and mother? Forty-nine times out of fifty, a wife will be the best qualified to keep the home. Biblically, she has the authority to keep the home and to care for her children (Titus 2:5). Mark it down, men are not best suited for this responsibility!

It's wonderful when a wife is willing to pitch-in and help with the finances by working outside the home. However, this arrangement is almost always second best. The home environment and the needs of children should remain her highest priority. Downsizing the financial requirement could be a better decision than taking a mother out of her home and away from her children. Why not choose a less expensive home, or car, or lifestyle? Usually nothing else works very well when the home is a scrambled, messed-up, disaster zone and the children are going wild. Tradition has it right; the wife is best suited to guide the home. It is a "sure-fire" reality that she is the only one qualified to birth a child and give it suck! God gave mothers the outstanding ability to nurture their children.

Showing "due consideration" for a wonderful wife is a must. We look out for her because her feminine nature is different from ours. The popular, bizarre, image that portrays women to be as strong as men is a "devilish lie." God did not give a woman the strength of a man. She is built a weaker vessel. That's the way she is designed to be. Human history provides a stirring testimony to the reality of how men have physically dominated women. One illustration of this is found in the following scripture:

> *Deuteronomy 22:28-29:*
> If a man find a damsel that is a virgin, which is not betrothed, and lay hold on her, and lie with her, and they be found; then the man that lay with her shall give unto the damsel's father fifty shekels of silver, and she shall be his wife; because he hath humbled her, he may not put her away all his days.

Simply put, men can force women sexually; women do not force men sexually. A woman's body is simply not built to equal the strength of a man's. So the next time you view a woman beating-up three men at one time on television you will know for sure this is a distortion of reality; it must be a lying devilish image.

The danger of such junkie imagery is that young women might be influenced to try and prove it true. It is not uncommon to see young women "pumping-iron" these days. There is nothing wrong with a woman building her body strength—it is okay for her to do so. However, when she "pumps-iron" to the point that she looses her femininity, that is another matter. The question is; what is her motivation in doing so? It is certainly not appealing from a man's prospective. (It "ain't" her muscles a man might like to feel.) Building her body out of proportion can become a perversion of her divinely given nature. Actually, she may become freaky looking.

It is the opposites between the sexes that are inviting. When we accentuate the differences between the sexes, men and women can delight in their differences. They were created as they are for a purpose. Our differences are meant to be appealing, inspiring, and uplifting. Our similarities give us a basic understanding of each other, but our differences need to be recognized, appreciated, and accentuated. Dan B. Allender makes the following comment in his book, *Intimate Allies*:

> As human beings we share so much in common; as males and females we are significantly and intriguingly different. The similarities are such that we can have a basic understanding of each other; the differences invite fascinating, unending exploration. It is an exploration that must lead to humbling awe and grateful praise to the God who thought up such wild diversity.[10]

It behooves us to search-out and to understand all we can about these differences. For example, a wife has a menstrual period—sometimes cramps and heavy bleeding become a part of it. In later years her monthly period will completely stop. Her body changes during pregnancy are phenomenal. Her emotional make-up is obviously more sensitive. Generally, she is more concerned with her

appearance than her husband might be of his. Indeed her
longer hair is a glory to her. We also need to learn, as
much as possible, about her mental make-up—the way she
thinks—what she likes and dislikes—what she is willing to
do and not do—what she is capable of doing, and what
might be more than she cares to handle. We need to learn
the intricacies of her personality and how best to motivate her. All this, and still there is much more to understand about her. The point here is that we deal with her
"according to knowledge." We put forth our best effort to
learn and understand her and the depth of her personality. Then, after we recognize how she is different from us,
we are careful to acknowledge, respect, and honor those
differences.

God honors both the nature of a man, and the nature of a
woman. Originally, He created both the male and female
in His image—God's image is <u>Spirit</u> (Genesis 1:27b), (John
4:24). When a husband and wife are born-again of God's
spirit they can, and should, share a rich and rewarding
prayer life. Their prayers are not going to be hindered
when they are mutually mindful of each other's God-given
position in the body of Christ. When they are faithfully carrying out their marriage vows, the blessing of the Lord will
be upon them, and answers to their prayers will abound.
The husband's function is to be the head of his wife, and
the wife gratifies her husband by her obedience. Respect,
consideration, and support for each other's marriage roles
are keys to their having a prosperous prayer life. They
are "heirs together of the grace of life." Together they
are "one flesh" and God's grace will rest upon the unity

of "their" marriage. Through steadfast agreement, and mutual believing, their prayers are established before God (I Peter 3:7).

Here is another wise directive:

Colossians 3:19:
Husbands, love your wives, and be not bitter against them.

That word "bitter" is talking about resentfulness. Husbands are not to allow what their wives say, or do, arouse them emotionally to the point of resentment. After all, she is made of flesh and blood, and is living in the same sin-stained world that he inhabits. Gary Thomas makes the following comments in his book entitled, *Sacred Marriage:*

In many of my seminars, I stress this over and over again: Husbands, you are married to a fallen woman in a broken world. Wives, you are married to a sinful man in a sinful world. It is guaranteed that your spouse will sin against you, disappoint you, and have physical limitations that will frustrate and sadden you. He may come home with the best of intentions and still lose his temper. She may have all of the desire but none of the energy. This is a fallen world. Let me repeat this: You will never find a spouse who is not affected in some way by the reality of the Fall. If you can't respect this spouse because she is prone to certain weaknesses, you will never be able to respect any spouse.[11]

Guard the atmosphere of peace that must be maintained between you and your wife. The honest thing to do is to lovingly confront matters that need to be confronted. It's counter-productive to allow things to build-up between the two of you. Just put other things on hold and deal with the most vital relationship you have—the well being of you and your spouse. Strife and discord are heavy weights to carry from one day to the next. Unsettled quarrels from today can mushroom into a full-fledged war by tomorrow. The following words from Ephesians 4 are addressed to any and all Christian Believers, so they most assuredly apply to the relationship between a husband and his wife.

Ephesians 4:31-32:
Let all bitterness, and wrath, and anger, and clamour, and evil speaking, be put away from you, with all malice: And be ye kind one to another, tenderhearted, forgiving one another, even as God for Christ's sake hath forgiven you.

Unresolved issues can become a sure deterrent to the health of any marriage union. Communicate, spend the necessary time to talk it out, and get those issues resolved. The Bible teaches that we are <u>not</u> to allow the sun to go down before we address and settle contentions and issues that arouse anger (Ephesians 4:26). No one likes confrontation, but confrontation is good for us if we are on a dangerous road and the bridge is out. See that any issue that might arise during the course of the day is settled in that same day. No matter how long it might take, stay with it until things are completely resolved. Wipe the slate clean, restore the peace, and then have a good night's sleep in each other's arms.

Below is another wise directive for a husband. It concerns faithfulness to his wife.

Proverbs 5:15-20:
Drink waters out of thine own cistern, and running waters out of thine own well. Let thy fountains be dispersed abroad, and rivers of waters in the streets. Let them be only thine own, and not strangers' with thee.
Let thy fountain be blessed: and rejoice with the wife of thy youth. Let her be as the loving hind and pleasant roe; let her breasts satisfy thee at all times; and be thou ravished always with her love. And why wilt thou, my son, be ravished with a strange woman, and embrace the bosom of a stranger?

George M. Lamsa's book, *Old Testament Light,* gives us the Eastern meaning of these verses:

This is an Eastern saying that is used commonly in vernacular speech and means "Love your own wife and keep away from other women." Water, in this instance, is symbolic of love between a husband and his wife and the children that are born to them [verses 17, 18]. "Drink waters out of thine own cistern, and running waters out of thine own well" means "Keep faithful to your own wife and have no relations with strange women."[12]

God will reward a husband's faithfulness to his wife. Sexual discipline and control starts in the heart and in the head. A Christian husband should discipline his mind to shut-off sexual fantasies about other women. A husband needs to keep his focus on his lovely wife, and rejoice in her beauty. This is a good way for him to stay out of trouble—not allowing the intrigues of other women to lure him away. He had plenty of time to search-out other women before his marriage. Those other women weren't so great before, why does he think that has changed? It hasn't! He should keep his mind and thoughts in check by having eyes for his beloved, only, and by exploring the depths of her beauty and goodness. Why not joy and rejoice in her, increasingly more, and more, year after year?

Yes, the enticement of beautiful women who adorn themselves in sensual attire is very common. Jesus dealt with this "allurement and lust" issue when he said, "Whosoever looketh on a woman to lust after her hath committed adultery with her already in his heart" (Matthew 5:28b). It's far better for a man to pour cold water on his lustful intentions than to pay the heavy, exacting price, which will come with an adulterous affair. It is certainly a bad decision for a husband to focus on that which is going to bring misery and destruction to his life! Fifteen minutes of pleasure, stacked-up against the loosing of a marriage, and lingering years of guilt, is a very bad decision for a man to make. One woman is enough for any man. A husband needs to stay contented with his wife's charms—she has plenty of them. Maybe he has not yet discovered them all.

Hebrews 13:4:
Marriage is honourable in all, and the bed undefiled: but whoremongers and adulterers God will judge.

Below is another directive. This is the last one we will address here. (There are other subjects that need to be discussed.)

Proverbs 31:10:
Who can find a virtuous woman? For her price is far above rubies.

Your bride is truly a gift from God. She's a prize! If she is a virtuous woman her price exceeds the worth of the biggest bank account. What an asset she is going to be to your life. It may take months and even years for you to fully recognize the depth of her worth. However, daily searching out the depth of her worth will keep your appreciation of her "up to par." Your thankfulness and appreciation of her should keep you highly motivated to be at your best. This beautiful woman belongs to you, and she has willingly entrusted her heart and life into your care and keeping. That's right, she has given her heart to you! She has done so because she believes that you are going to be a faithful man. One day on and the next day off just won't cut it with her. Living that way would be like the two of you taking a three-hour walk through the dark woods at night. The flashlight worked just fine for the first hour of the walk—you could see fine. Then suddenly the batteries start to lose their power and the light begins to flicker on and off. The next two hours are spent mostly groping around in darkness. Your consistent light of dependability will bless your woman.

Consistency is vital in a marriage. It's like the glue that holds things together. Think about how consistent God is.

> *Deuteronomy 7:9:*
> Know therefore that the Lord thy God, he is God, the faithful God, which keepeth covenant and mercy with them that love him and keep his commandments to a thousand generations.

God is not here today and gone tomorrow. We can count on Him to be there for us! This is surely the expectation of any normal wife for her husband. She relies upon the faithfulness of her husband's words and deeds. She can count on him and his consistency. He's not flashing on and off like a loosely screwed light bulb. His consistency brings stability to her life, and to the life-blood of their marriage. This is what she needs in her husband and this is what a godly husband will provide. He will set his mind to faithfulness, and he will not allow his priority to become distracted or shaken. His beautiful wife is like a "pearl of great price," and he's sold-out to holding her heart safely in his caring hands.

THE TRUE RICHES

It's up to us husbands to seek-out and apply these sparkling gems of marriage wisdom. God's Word contains the statues and judgments that are going to give us the guiding wisdom we need as husbands and fathers. It needs to be said again, the greatest assurance we men can give to our families emanate from being "sure-footed" in the spiritual categories of life. Our physical persona may inspire our wives for a little while, but our bodies are constantly corrupting. It is from our spiritual nature, and understanding that our wives and children will gain confidence in us and be encouraged by us. A husband can manifest tremendous confidence in his position as the head of his wife and family when his heart has determined to do what God says.

Again, our highest calling in life is to please our Heavenly Father. A man can make a fortune and still be a failure if he fails to please God. The riches of this life are not enough. The parable of the rich fool, whose farm had brought forth plentifully, is such a great example of this. Remember his conversation with himself?

Luke 12:17-21:
And he thought within himself, saying, What shall I do, because I have no room where to bestow my fruits? And he said, This will I do: I will pull down my barns, and build greater; and there will I bestow all my fruits and my goods. And I will say to my soul, Soul, thou hast much goods laid up for many years; take thine ease, eat, drink, and be merry.
But God said unto him, Thou fool, this night thy soul shall be required of thee: then whose shall those things be, which thou hast provided?
So is he that layeth up treasure for himself, and is not rich toward God.

119

The riches of this life pale before the riches of eternity. When we are rich toward God we can teach our wives and children the important spiritual values of life and living. When we are committed in our hearts to live as ambassadors of the Lord Jesus Christ, our families will be motivated to follow our example. What a legacy we are leaving to our families when they behold us serving the Bread of Life to the people of this world. We are teaching them how to be rich toward God. As Christian husbands, our godly calling is to feed our wives and children the true bread that came down from heaven, that they might eat of this bread and live with us in eternity (John 6:58).

Now it's certainly true that we husbands are not perfect. We are living in a corrupted world and in corruptible bodies—we remain sinners saved by the grace of God. We will make mistakes from time to time. Yes, we are going to fall short occasionally; however, with the sure standard of God's Matchless Word, alive in our hearts, we will get it right the vast majority of the time. It is also a sure reality that the spirit God has implanted within us is a "perfect spirit." We're renewing our minds daily to who we are in Christ Jesus, and to the spiritual power we are able to manifest. We are sons of God in the midst of this crooked world, and we are absolutely without rebuke (Philippians 2:15). Yes, He that lives in us is far greater than he (the devil) that lives in this world; God has directed us to the right road. We are on the road that leads to eternity. We know where we are going, and we are doing our very best to take our wives and children with us. See you there in heaven, Honey!

CHAPTER 5

WIVES AND THEIR HUSBANDS

❦

t is God that has given a woman her feminine qualities. He gave her different temperaments and inclinations than that of a man. God chose to make her a "weaker vessel" (physically). He designed her attractive, soft-flowing, body and gave her those nice inviting curves. The glory of her long hair is God-given. He gave her an almost unbelievable ability—the capacity to conceive and birth a child—and then to feed it with her milk. He gave her a higher pitched voice than that of a man—men generally find this inviting. Her motherly heart to lovingly care for her child is so outstanding. And yes, she was made to meet the needs of a loving husband, and by doing so, her needs are going to be met.

This beautiful creature God gave to Adam. Adam called her "Woman" because she was made from flesh taken from his body. God designed a woman in such a fashion that, in marriage, she meshes together with her husband—she is a compliment to his life. God did not make a woman to be a mate for another woman, nor did He design a woman to stand in opposition to a man. He did not make her to become the rugged individualist who carves out her own private agenda, no matter what her husband thinks. Nor did God give her the authority to rule her husband—she is not designed to take on the responsibility of leadership in her marriage.

Leadership authority over her husband is altogether foreign to what God had in mind. God had compatibility and companionship between a husband and his wife in mind when He instituted the union of marriage. This is what God did—He designed the marvelous way that a wife and her husband can blend together in an up-lifting union that compliments, completes, and fulfills, their lives together. It was God who made the decision to give a husband the authority to lovingly rule his wife, and for the wife to honor her husband's authority by submitting to him. This is exactly what the Bible teaches concerning the position of a wife in a marriage relationship. Not everyone accepts the biblical view—feminist sympathizers mock what the Bible teaches concerning the role of a wife.

TWO OPINIONS

Today, culturally, and also individually, we are being confronted with two views about the role of a wife in marriage. One is the biblical view, and the other is a perverted feminist view that emerged out of humanistic thinking. These two views are set in opposition to one another. Our job is to fully recognize the crippling distortion of the feminist view and then to wholeheartedly embrace what God teaches us concerning the role of a wife. It's important that we take the time to do this because the feminist view of marriage has gained so much acceptance (to our detriment) that it has become the prevailing standard in our culture. The first view we are going to examine is that of the feminists. (It will take several pages to present their history, growth and influence, but please stay patient; it will be worth your effort to read it.) After we have finished with what they teach and exemplify, we will examine a scripture-by-scripture account of what God teaches concerning the unchangeable role of a wife. To understand how the modern-day feminism movement got its start we will need to first look briefly at a doctrinal aspect of "humanism."

Natural-minded humanists champion only humanistic knowledge. This is why they reject the existence of God altogether—by their human logic they can not prove God. They have restricted themselves to "human logic" as their only means to reach conclusions about the entirety of life and existence. They have chosen to rely upon a philosophical, naturalistic, frame-of-reference for understanding.[13] They have also latched onto "social justice precepts" to establish a semblance of morality. Worldwide there are around five to six million people who align themselves with organizational structures that openly embrace fool-hearted God-rejection. The Bible helps us to understand how they reach their misguided, dark, conclusions.

I Corinthians 2:12-16:
Now we have received, not the spirit of the world, but the spirit which is of God; that we might know the things that are freely given to us of God. Which things also we speak, not in the words which man's wisdom teacheth, but which the Holy Ghost teacheth; comparing spiritual things with spiritual. But the natural man receiveth not the things of the Spirit of God: for they are foolishness unto him: neither can he know them, because they are spiritually discerned. But he that is spiritual judgeth all things, yet he himself is judged of no man. For who hath known the mind of the Lord, that he may instruct him? But we have the mind of Christ.

There it is in a nutshell! Natural-minded individuals just can not figure God out—they lack the capacity to do so. Their lack of spiritual savvy and understanding has led them to God-rejection.

By the end of the 1950s the Christian Community had withstood much of the open prominence humanists enjoyed throughout the first half of the 20th century. Back in the 1950s a horror movie entitled, *The Blob,* played in local theaters. The Blob was a giant- size glob of acid-like membrane that oozed around, seeking out human flesh to feed upon. If the door were shut to keep it out, it would ooze under the bottom of the door and continue to search out human flesh. Humanism is like that. When it was confronted in the 1950s it oozed under the door, so to speak, and took on a new face. Its new face became the feminist movement.

Just like humanism, the tenets of feminism are built upon prideful human logic, and its conclusions, which lead to God-rejection.

THE SEEDBED OF DISCONTENT

In the early 1960s the groundwork of the modern feminist movement commenced with a few discontented women who expressed and maintained a rebellious attitude towards the established standards of marriage. In this same time-frame, the male image of strength and stability was beginning to fade.[14] The declining masculinity among men in that era provided a void that gave the opportunity young feminist-minded women needed to advance their causes. Confessions of, "truth is relevant" and, "if it feels good do it" became the popular thinking in those days. The moral fiber and stability of the preceding generation soon faded away. Consequently, a woman could not continue to rely on the strength of a man who showed no strength. It's no wonder women turned away from the lack of masculine leadership. The blind cannot lead the blind; both will fall into the ditch. The loud voices of discontented women grew louder and louder throughout the decades of the 1960s and 1970s. They aimed their contempt at the empty void of male stability, leadership, and morality. And why not, "Where there is no vision, the people perish" (Proverbs 29:18a).

It needs to be said here, whether men like it or not, God placed the authority of rulership upon the shoulders of husbands. It is foolhardiness, fear, and weakness of character, which leads men to ignore this responsibility. They must rule their wives and children or else swallow the sour-tasting consequences. From the biblical perspective, that which is occurring with the position and status of women in marriage today, men are ultimately responsible. Men carry the responsibility for the fruition of their authority, and also for the lack of it.

History has shown us how ungodly men have abused their authority in the way they have ruled their wives. They have not used their authority in the way God intended. The tenets of a godly marriage call for a husband's tender love and kindness; even after the pattern of Christ's love for the church. God never did intend cruelty and abuse in marriage, nor did He intend the abdication of masculine authority. When husbands ignore their responsibility for godly leadership their wives will try to take up the slack of what their husbands have left undone. The failure of masculine authority gave plenty of room for the feminist movement to ferment and expand. The groundwork of the modern feminist movement was helped along by at least two categories of men. One was ungodly men who exercised selfish ambitions to use women for their own purposes, and secondly, by wimpy men lacking the stamina of a backbone.

EARLY FEMINIST LEADERSHIP

Most of the early "feminists" were young intellectuals who were already involved in the sexual revolution of that day—few of them were married. Loose sex and drugs, and a spirit of rebellion against the established social and political order, enticed college students to join in and partake— thousands of them did. The basic argument offered by early feminists alleged that marriage was oppressive for a woman. Marriage denied her the freedom she deserved to pursue a, supposedly, more gratifying and rewarding life, working outside the home in the business community. Supposedly, she needed her independence to attain personal meaning, wholeness, and equality.

Numerous books appeared in the decades of the 1960s and 70s that gave impetus to the, newly born feminist agenda. A few foundational works, like the following, set the stage for the commencement of their revolution: *The Feminine Mystique* by Betty Friedman, *The Church and The Second Sex* by Mary Daly, *The Dialectic of Sex* by Shulamith Firestone, and *Against Our Will* by Susan Brownmiuller. The basic thrust of these works, and others like them, sought to destroy the integrity of what the Bible teaches concerning marriage. Rather than trying to discredit the entirety of the Bible and what it teaches, they chose to slip in by the backdoor and attack what they called, the "male theology" of the Christian community.

The feminist argument was that Christian theologians were men. Because they were men their interpretation of the scriptures favored a masculine point of view. The feminists argued that they had a right to offer the feminine point of view in the interpretation of the Bible. And, offer it they did! Throughout the decades of the 1980s and 90s hardcore proponents of the feminist movement blatantly distorted what the Word of God teaches. In her book, *The Feminist Mistake,* Mary Kassian points out:

> Feminism does not present itself as an outright affront to the Bible, but it nevertheless contains an insidious distortion that erodes the authority of Scripture. Acceptance of the feminist thesis may not drastically alter one's initial beliefs, but if followed, it will naturally and logically lead to an end miles away from the Christianity of the Bible.[15]

Kassian reports that Rosemary Ruether and Letty Russell, two early feminist theologians, claimed that:

> A feminist liberation theology, which viewed liberation as the crux of the Bible, was the theological solution for the equality of women. [Kassian goes on to say] However, in choosing liberation, and more specifically the liberation of women, as the lens through which to interpret the Bible and contemporary events, they claimed the right to name themselves [i.e. their role in marriage and life as opposed to what the Bible teaches]. Instead of deciding what liberation and freedom meant according to the Bible they interpreted the Bible according to their preconceived definition of those terms.[16]

Sadly, Christian leadership did not stand up and successfully confront the lying assertions levied against them. Their failure allowed the "feminist snowball of discontent" to pick up momentum and grow in its size and influence.

PRIVATE INTERPRETATION OF THE BIBLE

The feminists supposed "right to interpret the Bible," in whatever way they chose, was essentially an out-of-control ego trip. They sought to analyze the gospel by measuring and comparing it with their personal experience. If their personal experiences were different than what the Bible taught, they negated the Word of God and then replaced it with their condescending personal conclusions. Their efforts to inject their agenda into the meaning of the Bible, were to say at the least, dishonest. In affect, they elevated themselves above the Bible and God Himself. They twisted the obvious meaning of the scriptures into what thy sought to prove. These misguided feminists were absolutely wrong about their right to interpret the Bible privately through feminist eyes. Nor do male theologians have a right to private interpretation of the scriptures. The Bible itself is crystal clear about this.

II Peter 1:20:
Knowing this first, that no prophecy of the scripture is of any private interpretation. For the prophecy came not in old time by the will of man: but holy men of God spake as they were moved by the Holy Ghost (Spirit).

The phrase "of any private interpretation" literally means, "of one's own interpretation." No one has the right to his own private opinion of what the Word of God teaches. Informed, honest, students of the Bible respect this important basic key to the understanding of all scripture. They have learned this important fundamental rule—the Bible interprets itself. About 80% of the biblical text is clearly understandable just as it is written—it says just what it means right in the verse as one reads it. The more difficult passages of the Bible require diligent study. However, the student of the scriptures, first and foremost, must understand in his heart that the Bible is not the words of men, but in truth, they are the Living Words God has given to men.

Recognition of this tremendous reality, that the Bible interprets itself, evokes respect, honor, and great honesty by those who are serious in their searching of the scriptures. But not with the feminists! Feminist theologians mocked God's Matchless Word by their homespun, private interpretation. Their perverted interpretations twisted the meaning of God's Word to support their personal agenda. The following is a small example of their twisted method of interpretation:

Joan Chamberlain Engelsman, in the *Feminine Dimension of the Divine* introduced the concept of a female divine persona in the Bible, Sophia. According to Engelsman, Sophia had traditionally been presented in the Bible as an allegoric figure named "Wisdom." *Sophia,* the Greek word for wisdom [or rather a transliteration of that word] immediately suggested a person rather than a concept, but Engelsman argued that this was precisely what the Bible had originally intended. She said that the translators' use of the title Wisdom rather than the name Sophia was a male ploy to avoid and repress this unique female deity. Engelsman, Susan Cady, Marian Ronan, and

Hal Taussisg, authors of *Wisdom's Feast,* wanted to see Sophia recognized as a real biblical deity.[17]

To deny what the Bible truly teaches, and then reconstruct it to say what you want it to say, is egotism in the extreme. Feminists made claims to nonexistent rights. Their feministic, prideful, arrogance was daring enough to undermine the living Word of God and replace its clear meaning with their out-of-bound human logic. This is exactly what radical feminism has done all along. Its egocentric teachings have essentially called God's Word a lie and what they propound about it to be truth.

After a while, the canon of God's Word became too confining for the radical feminists. They had been hampered all along by the teachings of the Bible. The next thing they did was to expand what they called valid scriptures. They could not distort the Bible enough to say what they wanted it to say, so they began to call upon outside sources of literature to justify their purposes.

In *Womanguides: Readings Toward a Feminist,* Rosemary Radford Ruether put together a series of texts and essays chosen from both biblical and nonbiblical texts. Her collection included writings from the ancient Near East, Hebrew and Greek mythology, Christian Science, paganism, goddess worship, and new "post-Christian consciousness." According to Ruether, anything that legitimized and recognized the full value of the female could be viewed as canonical.[18]

By expanding what they called scripture, feminists were able to redefine themselves in radically different ways. This is what they wanted to do all along. By renaming the role and purpose of a wife—by renaming the way a woman is to function in society—by renaming who a woman and a wife are they could function without, what they called, biblical restraints. So, they placed the relevance of the Bible, and thousands of years of tradition, behind their backs and chose to live according to the dictates of their own exalted personalities. They rebelled against the authority of a husband in marriage. They rebelled against the authority of cultural traditions. They rebelled against the authority of the Christian Community. Most importantly, they rebelled against our loving God and the authority of His Word. However, the justifications, by which radical feminists claimed their supposed liberation, are as unstable as a foggy morning. Why? Despite their philosophical assertions, they are functioning outside of their fullest potential--but even more importantly, they are functioning outside of the Word and Will of God.

The prideful conceit of the feminist movement eventually led to self-worship. Their goal had been to discover personal meaning for themselves as women. Feminist doctrine finally taught them to look within themselves for the answers for life and for their personal wholeness. By doing it this way, they could structure their own values and standards. This pathway led them directly to goddess worship. Once they had established their "right" to rename themselves, the world, and even God, they announced themselves to be the "ultimate authority" in this world, and in the universe. What followed this line of thinking was self-deification. The deification of her own essence has made the modern-day feminist a goddess to herself. She sees herself as "self-sufficient" in all aspects of life

- She herself now determines right and wrong, good and bad.
- She herself now determines what is reality and what is not.
- She herself now determines the rightful place of womanhood.
- She herself now determines the rightful role of marriage.
- She herself now determines the rightful role of relationships between men and women.
- She herself now determines the rightful role of women in the work place, and what it takes to facilitate her there.
- She herself now determines the rightfulness of lesbianism and homosexuality and same sex marriages.

Whatever she decides is right, in her own eyes, becomes right. That's the way it is. She's a goddess, end of the discussion. Of course, this is the height of prideful, misguided, self-love. It's almost unbelievable that the American Public and the Christian Community would swallow this odious logic; however, they have done so, almost without the blinking of an eye.

Feminism in its essence is an idolatrous practice. It is the worship of self—feminists, by in large, have left the God and Father of our Lord Jesus Christ out of their equation of life. Their having elevated womanhood to the status of god-ship is spiritual sick. The thrust of modern-day feminism from its start has been God-rejection. The feminist movement has not improved the status of women among our families and in our culture—it has diminished and frustrated womanhood, and the godly function of a wife in marriage. Feminism should, and must be, viewed for what it is—a corrupting evil.

UNSAVORY FEMINIST FRUITS

Just look at some of the unsavory fruit feminism has heaped upon us as individuals, and our society as a whole:

- They have generated antagonism, unrest, and strife between the sexes.
- They have motivated women to abandon their femininity and have fostered the anemic practices of the unisex.
- They have promoted lesbian-homosexual lifestyles and marriages.
- They have required the modification of the work place to facilitate their being a part of it.
- They have desperately tried to destroy the traditional wife's sense of self worth and fulfillment—they have been largely successful in this endeavor.
- They have glamorized vocational pursuits and scoffed at the importance of home and family life—actually, they have tried to destroy both the structure and

ultimately the institution of the family and replace it with their brand of disjointed individualism.

- They have insisted that equal status for a wife requires that she pursue a career with the same dedication as her husband—according to the feminist standard only a wage earner can be considered an equal marriage partner. (What narrow-minded illogic.)
- They have sought to lower-rate the ranking of motherhood in the eyes of society.
- They have sought to destroy the housewife's confidence that she is in fact engaged in an important and worthwhile enterprise for which she is uniquely qualified.
- They have brought a sense of bitterness, discontentment, and disappointment into the lives of young women who are not finding the feminist lifestyle all that it's proclaimed to be.
- They have amassed political power by having gained "minority rights status" and thereby they have worked their demoralizing agenda on the people of this nation.
- They helped to make no-fault state divorce laws a reality.
- They have established university and college women's studies curriculum to indoctrinate and perpetuate their misguided doctrines and beliefs.

One could easily fill another page or so listing all the unsavory fruits the feminist movement has smeared upon the face of American Society. There is no need to say more; enough has been said!

Feminist minded wives are going to have a difficult time finding the same contentment and fulfillment in the work place that they can enjoy in their homes and with their families. Their seeking the glory of the work place can be compared to the Children of Israel who exchanged their glorying after God and all His blessings for the deceiving vanity of bowing before a golden calf.

> *Psalm 106:19-21:*
> They made a calf in Horeb, and worshipped the molten image. Thus they changed their glory into the similitude of an ox that eateth grass. They forgat God their saviour, which had done great things in Egypt.

The Children of Israel exchanged the greater for the lesser—even for the empty and the vain. The glory of the home will always tower over the glory of the work place. The purpose of the work place is to fortify the home and family.

The fulfillment of the work place pales before the glory of giving birth and nurturing a son or a daughter. (On a personal note, I have worked in the work place for over forty years and let me tell you it "ain't" all that glorious in the first place.) The elusive priority of building a bank account and buying the trinkets of this world will never outweigh the rich rewards and benefits a wife will receive by tending to the needs of her husband and their children. Not because her husband is the greatest husband on the face of the Earth, but by doing so, she will be pleasing her Heavenly Father.

THE FEMINIST PLOY—DON'T SUBMIT

The thrust of feminist doctrine has built contempt of the Bible into the hearts of many modern-day wives. The feminist ploy is to trick a wife into questioning the validity of God's plan that asks a wife to submit to the authority of her husband. Today's liberal feminist sympathizers advocate that a so-called, "liberated wife" should not obey her husband. Submission to her husband, they say, is an "unfair expectation"—they say it's just not right to ask that of a wife. Actually, they foster the belief that she should, at the very minimum, share joint authority with her husband—or even better still, take control herself. They claim a husband does not support a wife's best interest, she must look out for herself.

The popularity of "feminist thinking" has younger wives viewing submission to their husband as an altogether outdated concept. Yes, they may even view submitting to be a demeaning expectation—by no means is it a necessary part of a wife's duty. These are just a few of the distorted arguments feminists make. Again, their plan of attack is to breed doubt and suspicion concerning the relevance of the Bible and the place it should occupy in the thinking of a wife. What they ask a wife to do opposes what God asks a wife to do.

The secular feminist method of attack continues to be an appeal to a woman's self-glorification. Younger women listen to secular feminist subtle arguments, and then begin to think: submission is indeed a hard road to travel, maybe that's asking too much of me; is it really "God's will" that I submit to this unappreciative husband of mine? I'm just as capable, and maybe I'm even more capable, of calling the shots in this marriage. The very day that a wife places her own word above the integrity of the Word of God, secular feminists rejoice. They rejoice because when a wife adopts their line of thinking she has rebelled against what God has asked her to do. In her rebellion, she has snuggled up to the enemy.

When a wife rebels against the biblical standard of marriage, all she can offer is lying evidence as a justification for her disobedience. She's allowed the thief to cheat her out of the pleasant fruit of obedience. Because of her rebellious spirit, fellowship with her Heavenly Father may be on a very rocky road. Her conceit has gotten the best of her. Her elevated self-image has gotten in the way of truth. She has fallen into the pit dug by our secularist culture. The road of disobedience she has chosen to travel will be difficult. It was paved with the egocentric cement of rebellion, contention, and strife. Just ask those who have already traveled this road—they will tell you that this treacherous roadway leads straight to a place called DIVORCE.

PLEASING GOD

A Christian wife must not allow the subtleties of feminism to enter into her mind and take root. Feminist teachings must not replace the certainty of God's Word in her thinking. Because God loves and cares for her so much, what He asks her to do will always be the best thing she can do for herself.

I John 5:3:
For this is the love of God, that we keep his commandments: and his commandments are not grievous.

The word "grievous" means burdensome. What God teaches a wife to do will never be a burden that she must endure. Just ahead, we will be looking into the biblical standard of submission. There we will find the depth of what God has to say about a wife's submission to her husband.

Pleasing God must come first for a wife, or anyone else in this life. If she gain the whole world and loose her "wifely soul" to making a fortune, she becomes the loser. It's not that a wife isn't qualified for the work place. She can drive a nail, pull a tooth, pilot a plane or run a corporation. She can do all of this and more. But in the end, it gets down to serving her higher purpose. Her purpose was established before she was born. She did not decide to be born and she cannot decide the purpose for her "wife-hood." Her purpose is God-given. He designed how she is to function. It is the fulfillment of her God-given role that will bring her the best she can have in life. (Know ye that the Lord He is God: it is He that hath made us, and not we ourselves. Psalm 100:3a) The big lie of the feminist movement is that there is a greater purpose in life for a wife and mother than giving herself to the care of her husband and children. The "lust of the flesh" and the "pride of life" are the beguiling appeals the feminists are utilizing to deceive her. The spiritual reality is that God gave a wife a vastly more important work than the glory and renown of a lofty career.

The horrific controversy between feminist doctrine and what God's Word teaches, is akin to what occurred with Eve in the Garden of Eden. The serpent (Satan) beguiled Eve. God's command was, do not eat fruit from the tree of the knowledge of good and evil that is in the midst of the garden. If she and her husband did so, God said they would die. Satan successfully led Eve to doubt the integrity of the Word of God.

> *Genesis 3:4-6:*
> And the serpent said unto the woman, Ye shall not surely die: For God doth know that in the day ye eat thereof, then your eyes shall be opened, and ye shall be as gods, knowing good and evil. And when the woman saw that the tree was good for food, and that it was pleasant to the eyes, and a tree to be desired to make one wise, she took of the fruit thereof, and did eat, and gave also unto her husband with her; and he did eat.

Eve, and her husband Adam, lost their spiritual connection with God the very day they rebelled against His Word. They suffered a spiritual death because they lost their spiritual nature. It's true, the devil (Mr. Slick), can offer you all the kingdoms of this world. However, his purpose has never changed—he continues to steal, kill, and destroy, (John

10:10b). He is working over-time in his efforts to foster God-rejection in our culture. The subtle, appealing promises that our feminist culture offers to women are very enticing, but so deceiving—they promise so much but deliver discord, misery, and unrest.

THE SECOND OPINION CONCERING THE ROLE OF A WIFE, THE BIBLICAL VIEW

The second opinion concerning the role of a wife is the biblical view—it is the right view. This view is not the view of a man. After all is said and done, the biblical view is God's view. He is its Author—it is His Word. He is the ultimate authority, we must answer to Him. It is fool-hearted for the clay to question the authority of the potter—"He is the potter and we are the clay." The opinions of men come and go, but God's Word is everlasting. What God has taught us about the role of a wife is not going to change. Cultures change because the opinions of men are constantly fluctuating. The immutable principles stated by the Word of God are eternal; they will never change.

This following Scripture-by-Scripture study is not intended to be just an academic exercise. It will take far more than just mental assent to assimilate these prudent Scriptures into daily living. They are not just casual, light-hearted thoughts that one may choose to do if they are appealing. Nor are they out-dated words that have lost their value and relevance. They are THE Precious Words of Life. They should become the life-blood of the relationship a wife shares with her husband. These are the very words that she must strive to trust and obey. The strength and power of what these words teach will enable her life. By the application of these words a wife can build a wonderful, sound, healthy marriage. The need is that she "let go and let God"—He will come through and stand beside her every time. She must not be swayed and tricked by the deceitful voices that call-out for her to rebel against her Heavenly Father—she is to treasure His Word. A Christian wife has the responsibility to control her thinking by keeping her focus on what God has to say.

Romans 12:1-2:
I beseech you therefore, brethren, by the mercies of God, that ye present your bodies a living sacrifice, holy, acceptable unto God, which is your reasonable service.
And be not conformed to this world: but be ye transformed by the renewing of your mind, that ye may prove what is that good, and acceptable, and perfect, will of God.

Each of the Scriptures used in this chapter deal with the responsibilities, duties, and privileges, of a wife. Some of them have been discussed in other chapters; however, here our emphasis is centered, more specifically, upon what God has to say to a wife.

WHY A WIFE?

The first Scripture reference we are going to study has to do with God's purpose in making a wife.

Genesis 2:18-20:
And the Lord God said, It is not good that the man should be alone; I will make him an help meet for him. And out of the ground the Lord God formed every beast of the field, and every fowl of the air; and brought them unto Adam to see what he would call them: and whatsoever Adam called every living creature, that was the name thereof. And Adam gave names to all cattle, and to the fowl of the air, and to every beast of the field; but for Adam there was not found an help meet for him.

Adam had a lofty work in naming the animals and keeping the Garden of Eden. He was a busy man and "in charge" before Eve arrived. However, he was living in loneliness without her presence—he was incomplete without her. These verses say it so well; Adam (man) was incomplete by himself. Without a woman his physical, mental, and emotional needs were not fulfilled. There was not another human with whom he could share his life. This is why God made a woman. God, whom had made Adam, knew exactly what it would take for Adam to reach his full potential. The term "help meet" in this verse needs a little explaining. This term in the Hebrew text is meant to convey the meaning of suitability. God made woman a "suitable" companion for Adam, one that would complete his physical, mental and emotional needs by being his helper. God made both a man, and his wife, so they are able to compliment each other. They are so designed that they can fulfill each other's needs. The why of a woman's creation is that a man is incomplete without her—he is in need of her help, and her need is to be a help to him. The means by which they achieve their completeness is the God-ordained union of marriage.

MEETING HIS NEEDS

What we need to understand is how a wife is designed to meet the needs of her husband, and thereby make him complete. This must be her purpose in marriage, and it will need to be set in her heart in order for her to achieve it. Following a different image for her role in marriage will lead to confusion and dismay. We know already that she is made with the capacity to be a blessing—she is the "suitable mate" of God's design. When she is meeting the physical, mental, and emotional needs of her husband, her life is rich because she is accomplishing her purpose. And, it works both ways—a husband's fulfillment comes by completing the needs of his wife. Their ability to meet each other's needs is the attraction that draws them together. Meeting each other's needs gives them completeness.

A wife's capacity to meet the needs of her husband is indeed so outstanding—it is even astonishing. What she brings to the life of her husband is an endowment fashioned by God Himself. By working at it she can become a helper beyond belief! In general terms, here are just a few of the tremendous attributes and benefits that a wife can bring to her husband:

- Her beauty is an inspiration to him— she's a treasure to behold.

- To be loved and respected by a beautiful woman heightens a man's self image—she pumps him up and makes him feel even more important.
- The positive encouragement of her words brings reinforcement to his life.
- She brings joy to her man because they can share their victories and accomplishments.
- Her friendship makes him a rich man.
- Her tenderness brings warmth and inspiration.
- Her gentleness qualifies her to mother children.
- Her sensitivity, industriousness, and imagination enable her to make their home a place of comfort and beauty—she is, in fact, the best qualified to take care of their home and their children.
- Her intelligence is always a plus.
- Her companionship is indispensable.
- Her point-of-view, her perspective brings an entirely new dimension of understanding to her man.
- Her presence is encouraging and her understanding of his life is a comfort.
- Her sexual propensities are intriguing, fascinating, and alluring—she brings sexual fulfillment to her husband—a playmate *par-excellence.*
- Her valuable support backs-up his endeavors, she is his suitable helper.
- A wise woman's counsel will make her husband all the wiser.

A wife is capable of this and much, much, more. A man becomes more than he could ever be without her—she's priceless. It would take a very large book to say all that could be said about the wonderful heart and life of a giving wife.

LETTING EGOTISM GO

Egotism is a detriment to a married couple's well being. In marriage, they must get their minds off of accentuating themselves, and instead, focus on being a blessing to their mate. They are dependent on each other for their whole-ness—together, as husband and wife, they make each other complete.

By the way, no where in the Bible are we taught to live a life of self-gratification; the very opposite is true. We are taught to serve our God, and we do so by serving the Bread of Life to a lost and dying world. We serve God by serving His people. Yes, husbands and wives absolutely fit into the category of people. It is by her generous giving that a wife blesses her needy husband—and he needs just what she has to offer. He's empty and lonely without what she brings to him. It is the work of a wife's hand that will elevate her husband. A Christian Believing wife must learn to let go of an exalted self-image to have success in marriage. She must take her focus off herself and give her energies to meeting the needs of her mate. This is true because she's God's gift to her husband. In her book, *Created To Be His Help Meet*, Debi Pearl describes the way she functions with her husband, Michael.

I never have a chip on my shoulder, no matter how offended I have a right to be—and I do have reasons to be offended regularly. Every day, I remember to view myself as the woman God gave this man. This mind-set helps me be just that: a gift, a playmate, his helper.[19]

Mrs. Pearl has certainly captured God's heart in the way she views her relationship with her husband. In marriage, the critical impact of the individual's life is what he or she can bring to the table—what they have to <u>give</u>. When a husband and his bride have their minds set on how they can be a blessing to each other, their thinking harmonizes with God's plan, and purpose, for their marriage—God made them, each for the other. It is through the mutual giving of themselves that their needs are going to be fulfilled. When the two of them are doing it right, their giving is reciprocal. What they are giving to one another reverberates back in a very gratifying manner. God-ordained-equality can only come by the fulfillment of mutual giving. When both the husband and the wife are giving, and both are receiving, there is equality.

BUILT TO BE A GIVER

A wife is to give from the abundance of her abilities. She is built to be a giver. And, it is by the fruits of her giving that she will receive from her husband's storehouse of treasures. It is her "gift of obedience" that will help to generate, in him, thankfulness and gratitude, respect, and appreciation for her life. It is her giving that activates his response to share with her what he has to offer.

Proverbs 31:11-12:
The heart of her husband doth safely trust in her, so that he shall have no need of spoil. She will do him good and not evil all the days of her life.

Submission is the means by which a wife offers the storehouse of her abilities to her husband. Her obedience is like the offering of a sacrifice. Her sacrificial willingness to obey becomes the glorious proof, the living reality, of her deep-seated love and respect for her man. Her obedience becomes to him, an almost unspeakable gift—he becomes fully persuaded of her love. Her giving will inspire his trust and confidence. It is the act of the "giving of herself" to her husband that becomes her golden key. With this golden key she can open the treasure box of her husband's heart and receive from him just what she needs to make herself complete in life. Neither of them is self-sufficient. They are incomplete without what each one gives to the other. He needs her beauty, her charm, her grace, her submission and support. She needs his loving guidance, his supply and protection, and the other treasures he is able to provide for her life.

THE HIGH STANDARD OF GIVING

The high potential of what a godly wife has to offer is outlined for us in the thirty-first chapter of Proverbs. It is "reverence of God" in the heart and life of a wife that will motivate her to become the virtuous woman described here—this is truly a high meritorious standard for a wife to achieve. God's Word always calls out the best in us. From the following passage of Scripture you are going to see a virtuous woman who's heart is focused on what she can do to bless her husband and her family. Gentlemen, if you have a godly wife like the one described here, you are indeed abundantly blessed, "for her price is far above rubies."

Proverbs 31:
Vs. 11-12: The heart of her husband doth safely trust in her, so that he shall have no need of spoil. She will do him good and not evil all the days of her life.

The above Scripture was addressed earlier; however, another aspect of these two verses needs to be understood. A man does not need competition from his wife; he needs her comfort, her support, and her encouragement. He needs to be persuaded about her unshakable confidence in him and in his ability to lead, protect, and provide. If a wife gives him unwarranted feedback by constantly questioning his decisions, he is going to have a problem with that. In effect, her questions will say to him, "I don't think you know what you are doing." This is the very opposite of what he needs to hear from his wife. What he needs to hear from her is, "You make good decisions, Honey. I trust you, and I am so thankful for your tremendous leadership." He will thrive on words like these. When he makes a bad decision, as he will from time to time, what he needs to hear is, "Honey, you may have been mistaken about this situation but I still trust you. I know your heart was in the right place, despite this mistake. You are a very good leader. You can count on my support. I think you are great, you are the best there is." When he hears encouraging words like these, a husband's heart can safely trust in his wife's loyal support.

I published this song a few years ago. It is entitled, *My Virtuous Woman*. The sentiment of this song expresses some of what a husband needs and enjoys from his wife.

> My virtuous woman strengthens my soul.
> Her grace and beauty, her giving I behold.
> Her pleasant voice encourages me.
> I must be in heaven; where else could I be?
> I must be in heaven; where else could I be?
>
> My heart's deepest longings she understands.
> I safely trust the good works of her hands.
> Her warm heart's key she's given to me.
> I must be in heaven; where else could I be?
> I must be in heaven; where else could I be?
>
> Her price above rubies, silver and gold,
> She's kind and loving, a beauty to behold.
> She's a blessing, a treasure to me.
> I must be in heaven; where else could I be?
> I must be in heaven; where else could I be?
>
> My beautiful woman, calling my name.
> Sweet wine and roses, I'll never be the same.
> Her tender eyes are smiling at me.

I must be in heaven; where else could I be?
I must be in heaven; where else could I be?[20]

The tender eyes of his wife smiling at him is big time "stuff" to a man—he needs that. Her smiles and twinkling eyes reassure him. They can make him feel like he is a king. Her support validates his opinion of himself. Her praise and encouragement under-girds him emotionally. Her willingness to back him up will bring a sense of gratification and pride to his heart.

The phrase above in Proverbs 31:11, "so that he shall have no need of spoil," refers to how this virtuous wife adequately furnishes her husband in every way. There is no need to go to other sources; she fully supplies his needs. In other words, she is every thing he needs! She shares her life with him fully. She brings sexual fulfillment to his life. She is his wonderful helper and companion. She supports him in every way; physically, emotionally, mentally, and also spiritually. Her intent is to bless his life. She comforts and encourages him. No wonder he can confidently trust in her.

Vs. 13-16:
She seeketh wool, and flax, and worketh willingly with her hands.
She is like the merchants' ships; she bringeth her food from afar.
She riseth also while it is yet night, and giveth meat to her household, and a portion to her maidens. She considereth a field, and buyeth it: with the fruit of her hands she planteth a vineyard.

These verses pinpoint the industriousness of this wife. She is a "get-up-and-go" kind of lady. Her first concern is the welfare of her family. She willingly takes on the responsibility of clothing and feeding them. Today, the merchant's ship is as close as the grocery store. But, economy, thoughtfulness, and imagination in her shopping and household duties show how capable she manages. It is obvious; she is willing to give what it takes to get the job done.

Do not get misled by Old Testament cultural practices in this reference to buying a field. God's Word is not asking wives to get into the real estate business. The emphasis here is on this wife's fruitfulness. She makes wise financial decisions for her family. No impulsive spending by this woman; she thinks about it carefully before she makes a buying decision. A wife today might choose to purchase a new refrigerator with her savings.

Vs. 17-19:
She girdeth her loins with strength, and strengtheneth her arms. She perceiveth that her merchandise is good: her candle goeth not out by night. She layeth her hands to the spindle, and her hands hold the distaff.

This virtuous wife takes care of herself physically. She maintains her health and her poise. It takes physical stamina to care for the needs of the family, and she is up to the task. Her work goes on into the night.

V. 20-21:
She stretcheth out her hand to the poor; yea, she reacheth forth her hands to the needy. She is not afraid of the snow for her household: for all her household are clothed with scarlet.

The fruits of her labor have provided her with the finances to bless the poor. She has to give to those who need (Ephesians 4:28). The fruit of her labor has provided warm and attractive garments for her family. She has prepared them for the cold of winter.

V. 22:
She maketh herself coverings of tapestry; her clothing is silk and purple.

Not just any old bedspread will do—not just any old cushion to sit upon—not just any old dress to wear; this virtuous wife provided a beautiful bedspread, a fancy cushion to sit upon, and a beautiful dress to wear.

V. 23:
Her husband is known in the gates, when he sitteth among the elders of the land.

Her husband was a man of distinction; respected by the people in his community. He "sat among the elders" means he helped in the governmental affairs of his town. His virtuous wife cared for his needs. Her support was an aid to his stature and standing in their community. She shared in his reputation and rejoiced in his accomplishments.

V. 24:
She maketh fine linen, and selleth it; and delivereth girdles unto the merchant.

This verse is not advocating that a modern Christian wife starts a home-based business. In the biblical culture of the Near East skilful, industrious wives would work in their spare time for the niceties they desired for themselves, their children, and their husbands. The emphasis here in this verse is upon the productive skill of a virtuous wife. She is not sitting idly by and wasting her time, but is productive in providing niceties for her family to enjoy.[21]

Vs. 25-27:
Strength and honour are her clothing; and she shall rejoice in time to come. She openeth her mouth with wisdom; and in her tongue is the law of kindness. She looketh well to the ways of her household, and eateth not the bread of idleness.

The description of this virtuous woman's life is now more inward. These two verses are like the apex of a crescendo. They are describing the high standing of her inner nature— the inner woman of her heart. The moral fiber of this wife is outstanding. She has the inner strength to do what is required of her and from her. The beauty of her outward appearance comes from what she wears on the inside. Her inner attire is her strength and stamina to "do him good."

It is her heart to "do him good" that brings honor to her life. She maintains a positive frame of mind about the future. Her expectation is that good days are coming.

The fear of the Lord is the beginning of wisdom (Psalm 111:10). In verse 30 of this chapter this virtuous wife is described as a " woman that feareth [respects] the Lord." When she broke the silence of her mouth, she spoke from the wisdom of the Lord. The wisdom of the Lord resided in the depth of her heart. Her life, and the work of her hands, exemplified the wisdom that was in her heart. This is behavior that is becoming to a wife in any age and time. Any marriage will benefit when a wife's heart is focused upon the Word of the Lord and she lives by its wisdom.

Here is a personal note for wives. I would like to point out that what is taught by this proverb is vital to a good marriage. The ageless instruction of this proverb calls out today, to women who are born-again, "Let My teaching become the wisdom of your thinking and your behavior." For it is by the power of God's Word, at work in the depth of your heart, that you will gain the wisdom needed to direct your marriage. Let its enlightenment give you the wisdom to understand the great need of your presence in your home. Let its enlightenment give you the wisdom to understand the importance of what you can do to turn a house into a home. Let its enlightenment give you the wisdom to see your Heavenly-appointed place in marriage and the courage and grace to faithfully do what is required of you. Let its enlightenment give you the wisdom to understand the needs of your children and what you must do to meet those needs. Let the light of God's Word give you the wisdom to understand the importance of meekness towards your husband and why you need to submit to his leadership.

The focus and activity of this virtuous woman was upon her duty to her family. The success of her family depended on her loving care for them. The children needed to be fed and clothed. Their father needed his suit pressed. The garden needed to be tended. The family budget needed to be adjusted. Company was coming tonight, and she needed to prepare for them. There was much to do and a lazy wife would falter. The bread of idleness would not get the job done. A lazy wife would fail to meet the needs of the people who were counting on her the most, her family.

V. 28-29:
Her children arise up, and call her blessed; her husband also, and he praiseth her. Many daughters have done virtuously, but thou excellest them all.

My grandmother, May Johnston, was a giving, caring, loving woman. She gave birth to eight children. As an adult, whenever I heard my father and his brothers and sister talk about their mother, they always had a sparkle in their eye and their voice projected reverence. They talked about her giving generosity and her kindness. They talked about the loving care she showed to them and the way she pampered and cared for their father. They were so thankful for all their mother had done for them. They "rose up and called her blessed." My grandmother lived in a farmhouse that was cold in the winter, and hot in the summertime. She never had many modern conveniences. She was in her late 50s when finally they put in an indoor toilet. She never owned a diamond ring. She never had fancy furniture. She managed with what her husband provided and was content with what she had. But oh, how rich she was! She had the praise of her sons and her daughter and her husband. Her children honored her, and they respected her. They rejoiced in her goodness and in the love she had shown to them in their youth. Their joy, their praise, their honor and reverence and their admiration were the most valuable things my grandmother ever possessed. There was nothing in this world that could have over- shadowed the joy and satisfaction she received from her family. And, what could be more valuable to a mother and a wife; what greater treasure could she possess?

The virtuous woman in this acrostic song of Proverbs 31 deserved to be praised. She had earned it! Her children rose up and praised her, but so did her husband. As a matter of fact, he said that though there are many women around who might make good wives, his wife excelled them all. She was #1 in his eyes. No other women out-classed his wife. And, what wife would not like her husband to think this highly of her?

Vs. 30-31:
Favour is deceitful, and beauty is vain: but a woman that feareth the Lord, she shall be praised. Give her of the fruit of her hands; and let her own works praise her in the gates.

The fleshy standards of charm and beauty are shallow and fleeting. These worldly values fade away quickly. The promises of God are rich and enduring. They will last throughout eternity. God's Word says that a woman who honors Him shall be praised. This is a promise that any wife can take to the bank—it <u>shall</u> absolutely come to pass!

This tremendous passage of scripture ends with the notation, "let her own works praise her in the gates." A virtuous wife will absolutely gain the praise she has earned. She certainly deserves praise because she has chosen to please her husband and her family, and in doing so, she has pleased her Heavenly Father. Her priorities were straight—she was living an agenda of God's design. Her ambition was not to promote her self-interest. It wasn't "herself" that she sought to exalt. Her ambition was rather the heart of a loving servant—she wanted the best for every member of her family. Her loving heart was willing to give all that it took to meet their needs.

Matthew 23:11-12:
He that is greatest among you shall be your servant.
And whosoever shall exalt himself shall be abased;
and he that shall humble himself shall be exalted.

We have already seen what distorted feministic thinking asks of a wife. How it asks that she "exalt herself" by redefining her role as a wife differently than the way God teaches her to function. However, that which is promised by self-gratification is only an illusion, it's deceptive. It is a deceiving falsehood that "she who exalts herself will be better off." After any honest searching of the Scriptures the conclusion concerning the rightful role of a wife must be that her "ministry" in marriage is to see to the needs of her husband. Thusly, her rightful choice is to glory in a life of loving service to her husband and their family. A wife should absolutely view her relationship with her husband as a ministry. Truly, this is just what God has in mind for her. God's plan is for her to meet the needs of her husband, and that certainly will require the task of ministering to him. Loving service may even require putting his needs before her own.

I Corinthians 7:34b:
But she that is married careth for the things of the world, how she may please her husband.

There are two ways of looking at marriage. The "world's view" of marriage pictures what you might expect to get out of it—primarily how it is going to benefit you. The "heavenly view" of marriage is quite different from that. The God-ordained view of marriage is that of a loving heart to give—what can I give to bless my mate?

It is from the outstanding biblical principle of giving that a wife can learn about the rich success that awaits her in marriage. She comes fully equipped with tremendous abilities, with treasures, with everything that is needed to satisfy and supplement her husband. If she is a smart woman she will become a cheerful, hilarious giver, even a reckless giver of her endowment. Our Lord Jesus Christ has taught us so plainly that, "IT IS MORE BLESSED TO GIVE THAN TO RECEIVE" (Acts 20:35b).

A UNIVERSAL LAW

As a wife gives to meet the needs of her husband, his heart can grow in thankfulness and appreciation of what she brings to his life. He will value her all the more. The benefits of her having "given to him" will outweigh what she has personally sacrificed in doing so. She is, after all, "giving from her sufficiency"—she has to give to him that needs (Ephesians 4:28b). What she is going to receive by having done so is an "exalted reward." She is going to receive a greater benefit than what she has given. Her giving will be multiplied back to her. This is the way it works, and it works for everyone the same. This is what God has established by His universal law of giving and receiving. The law of giving and receiving is a spiritual principal. From a human logic point-of-view it makes no sense—how can one have more by giving away what they have? Here in the context of marriage relationships it is easy to see that those whom have choose to become loving, cheerful givers to their mates have built solid gratifying marriages. Those whom are selfish, or "meter-out" their giving, are the ones who struggle in sinking-sand marriages.

Wives, please let me point out that you have already decided your husband is a good investment. That is why you married him in the first place. So now you need to be especially forward in your giving to him. The greater your investment, the greater your return will be. The more you sow, the more you will reap in any category of life. So, be very generous with the seeds of blessing you sow into your husband's life. Fill him up with your helpfulness. Give him the full measure of your support. Your seeds of service, respect, adoration and submission are going to bring a bountiful harvest to your life. Remember that joyfulness is the reward for a willing mind to give!

II Corinthians 9:6-7:
But this I say, He which soweth sparingly shall reap also sparingly; and he which soweth bountifully shall reap also bountifully. Every man according as he purposeth in his heart, so let him give; not grudgingly, or of necessity: for God loveth a cheerful giver.

The life of our Lord Jesus Christ is the perfect example of what has been presented in our study of giving. He humbled himself in obedience to God's Word, and God has highly exalted him and has given him a name above ever name.

Philippians 2:3-5; 8b-11:
Let nothing be done through strife or vainglory; but in lowliness of mind let each esteem other better than themselves. Look not every man on his own things, but every man also on the things of others. Let this mind be in you, which was also in Christ Jesus: He humbled himself, and became obedient unto death, even the death of the cross. Wherefore God also hath highly exalted him, and given him a name which is above every name: That at the name of Jesus every knee should bow, of things in heaven, and things in earth, and things under the earth; And that every tongue should confess that Jesus Christ is Lord, to the glory of God the Father.

SUBMISSION

Who knows better than God does? He knows husbands and wives better than they know themselves. Yes, He understands the totality of the woman He's made. He knows the number of hairs on her lovely head. He knows the best way for a wife to function in her marriage. A wife was designed to be a wonderful helpmate for her husband, and God has determined that submission is for her best welfare. It is for this reason she will prosper by submitting to her spouse. Once a wife realizes that submission is first and foremost for her personal profit, her resolve to obey her husband can increase. No one can force her into obedience. Her response to the "Word of the Lord" is a personal decision. She, by her freedom of will, must choose to lovingly submit to her husband. Once she gets her will lined up with the Will of her Heavenly Father she is on the road to a prosperous, fulfilling marriage.

Proverbs 3:5-6:
Trust in the lord with all thine heart; and lean not unto thine own understanding. In all thy ways acknowledge him, and he shall direct thy paths.

Pleasing God remains the greatest accomplishment in life. If an individual pleases everyone else, and fails to please Him they become the poorer. Pleasing God is living victoriously. Doing the will of the Lord opens up the storehouse of His abundant blessings. A loving wife, who is submissive to her husband, will enjoy the blessings of her Heavenly

Father—they will rain-down daily. The inner peace of knowing that God is smiling upon her marriage will bring satisfaction and contentment that cannot come by any other means. A wife's decision to submit to her husband is a little like the parable Jesus gave of the talents delivered to servants by their steward. The wise servant who had the ability to manage five talents of silver invested the talents he had received and gained another five by the time his lord had returned. Because of that servant's faithfulness to use what he had been given his master made him ruler over many things. He was able to enter into the joy of his lord. God has endowed a woman with just what she needs to bless her husband. He has given her at least five talents. The wise woman, who happily invests her abilities into lovingly submitting to her husband, will receive the joyous rewards God promised a faithful wife. She will enter into the joy of her Lord. He will reward her faithfulness!

WORLDLY AUTHORITY OR LOVING SERVICE

Before we get into specific Scriptures concerning "submission" we need to look at the biblical view of authority. Submission, in the union of marriage, must be viewed in its relationship to authority. The Bible describes two kinds of authority. One is the authority exemplified by the lords of the world. This type of authority expresses itself by control, or force. A harsh boss or a tyrannical government is an example of this kind of authority. Jesus Christ referred to this kind of authority in a teaching he gave to the twelve apostles.

Matthew 20:25:
But Jesus called them unto him, and said, Ye know that the princes of the Gentiles exercise dominion over them, and they that are great exercise authority upon them ["them" refers to those who were in subjection to the power of the Gentile princes].

This is the kind of authoritative power two of his apostles were seeking. Their desire was to be seated on the right-hand and left-hand of Jesus Christ when he established his kingdom. Jesus wanted them to understand that authority or rulership in his kingdom differs greatly from how the people of this world exercise authority. Lording power over others is a worldly practice. However, ministering to the needs of others will be the standard of greatness in the kingdom of Jesus Christ.

Matthew 20:26-28:
But it shall not be so among you: but whosoever will be great among you let him be your minister; And whosoever will be chief among you, let him be your servant: Even as the Son of man came not to be ministered unto, but to minister, and to give his life a ransom for many.

On another occasion Jesus demonstrated the important principle of loving service to his apostles. This occasion was to be the last meal Jesus would share with them. After supper had ended he performed the duty of a household servant by taking a basin of water and a towel, and kneeling down, he washed the feet of his disciples. He was their

Lord and Savior, and yet he knelt down and washed their feet.

John 13:12-15:
So after he had washed their feet, and had taken his garments, and was set down again, he said unto them, Know ye what I have done to you? Ye call me Master and Lord: and ye say well; for so I am. If I then, your Lord and Master, have washed your feet; ye also ought to wash one another's feet [provide loving service to each other]. For I have given you an example, that ye should do as I have done to you.

The general notion that people have regarding the authority of a husband in marriage is faulty. It is mistakenly based upon the worldly standard of authoritative rule. The image of a husband exercising his power to force his will upon his wife cannot be found in the pages of the Bible. It is strictly a mistaken worldview that suggests a husband has the right to demand obedience from his wife. He may demand it, but that's not the way he is going to get it! The biblical authority of a husband is that of a love relationship. By his love, he is to woo his wife—his kindness and affection draws out her obedience. His lordship is to be that of loving service to guide his wife and to meet her needs. Her well being is his responsible. The love he has for his wife is to be after the pattern of the love Jesus Christ has for the church. And now, armed with this clear biblical understanding of what a husband's authority <u>is</u>, we can commence to study what the Bible has to say about a wife's submission duties and responsibilities.

BIBICAL SUBMISSION, VERSE BY VERSE

We have referred to the topic of submission several times already; however, because of its critical importance in the role of a wife we are going to study it in more depth. We will be looking at those verses in the Bible that asks a wife to submit to her husband. (They will appear in bold print.) There are at least six references in the scriptures that ask a wife to submit. The Greek word, *hupotasso*, is used in each of the six references. This word *hupotasso* appears 35 times in the New Testament and is always translated in one of three ways—subject—submit—or obedient. Its most basic meaning is "to set in array under"—to subject. A brief word is in order concerning the different connotations between the words submit and obey. Obedience can come from the head or from the heart. For example, it's possible to obey the laws of this land, and yet, down deep in the heart, resent having to do so. Biblically, submission is something that occurs in the heart. It involves the purposeful and trusting decision to yield one's will to another's authority. Obedience from the heart is on a higher plane than obedience that is required or demanded. The verses following show some of this decision process.

Romans 6:12-13;16-18:
Let not sin therefore reign in your mortal body, that ye should obey it in the lusts thereof. Neither yield ye your members as instruments of unrighteousness unto sin: but yield yourselves unto God, as those that are alive from the dead, and your members as instruments of righteousness unto God.

Know ye not, that to whom ye yield yourselves servants
to obey, his servants ye are to whom ye obey; whether
of sin unto death, or of obedience unto righteousness? But God be thanked, that ye were the servants
of sin, but ye have obeyed from the heart that form of
doctrine which was delivered you. Being then made
free from sin, ye became the servants of righteousness.

It is by obedience from a submissive heart, to the Word of
God, that we are freed from the bondage of sin. Obedience
to the Word of God from the "submissive heart" of a wife is
a fundamental key to her having a great marriage.

In the Scripture below, the word "submitting" is used in
the sense of military rank. (The way an army is organized
according to levels of rank. See *Strong's Concordance*[22]) In
the military, one is obligated to respect those of higher
rank—as a private would submit to a general. It is the office
of the general to which a private submits more so than to
the individual—rank has to do with the order of authority.
The context for the following scripture from the book of
Ephesians shows how God has established various spheres
of authority, and how Christian Believers are to honor them.

Ephesians 5:21-22:
**Submitting yourselves one to another in the fear of
God. Wives, submit yourselves unto your own hus-
bands, as unto the Lord.**

These verses need to be discussed together as a unit. Here,
"submission to one another in the fear of the Lord" refers

to the relationship we are to share with our brothers and sisters in Christ. We serve one another in the love of Christ. We respect each other for who we are. We are all <u>fellow members</u> of the body of Christ. The way we submit to one another as brothers and sisters in Christ Jesus is by loving service to each other. The voice of authority, to which brethren in Christ submit, is the voice of the Word of God. It is the voice of God's Word that teaches us how to behave towards one another, and we obey what God tells us to do. God is always the ultimate authority. There is no authority or power greater than God's.

Romans 13:1:
Let every soul be subject unto the higher powers. For there is no power but of God: the powers that be are ordained of God.

All authority belongs to God. He empowers men and women who have a heart to serve Him. In the Old Testament, God authorized the ministry of the prophets to speak on His behalf. They manifested the power God had given them by their words and deeds. When those men spoke they spoke on behalf of the Lord God of Heaven and Earth. When men and women respected the prophet's God-given authority and obeyed what they taught, <u>then</u> they profited. Failure to obey the Word of the Lord always produces a negative outcome. Both the nations of Israel and Judah disobeyed the message God had sent them through His prophets. The result of their disobedience was captivity. The Assyrians and Babylonians enslaved Israel and Judah for seventy years.

In the New Testament, God gave gift ministries to the church. They are our pastors, prophets, teachers, apostles, and evangelists. God ordained these ministries to function on His behalf. He has empowered them with the presence of His spirit. He has given to them the authority of leadership to serve the body of Christ, the Church. The premise upon which these ministries are to function is the authority of loving service. It is true that church leadership sometimes functions more like the authoritative practices of the lords of the world. But this is, of course, out of step with what God teaches them to do. The proper way the gift ministries are to function is in the power of God's spirit ministered by loving service to the body of Christ.

> *I Peter 5:1-3:*
> The elders which are among you I exhort, who am also an elder, and a witness of the sufferings of Christ, and also a partaker of the glory that shall be revealed: Feed the flock of God which is among you, taking the oversight thereof, not by constraint, but willingly; not for filthy lucre, but of a ready mind; Neither as being lords over God's heritage, but being ensamples to the flock.

The work of the gift ministries is for the perfecting of the saints, to build us up in our Christian walk. The authority that has been placed upon the gift ministries is for our good, to edification. Their work is to enable us by helping us to grow-up to the measure of the stature of the fullness of Christ (Ephesians 4:11-13). However, the work of the gift ministries will not profit in the face of disobedience.

Obedience to their leadership is a must! Without the response of obedience, on the part of men and women in the church, there will be little or no growth. It takes our submission, our "doing the will of the Lord," to get the benefits He has promised to us. Submission to His ministers will prosper our lives. Obedience to their leadership will produce growth in us towards the likeness of Jesus Christ.

Hebrews 13:17:
Obey them that have the rule over you, and submit yourselves: for they watch for your souls, as they that must give account, that they may do it with joy, and not with grief: for that is unprofitable for you.

Submission to God, and to the people in whom He has placed authority, is the critical behavior that will bring success to the life of any Christian Believer—married or living alone. Submission to the word of the prophets in the Old Testament brought success. Submission to the gift ministries of the New Testament brings success. Submission on the part of a wife to the leadership of her husband will help to bring uplifting success to their marriage. When a wife acknowledges that the "Word of the Lord" has established her husband's leadership authority, her believing can then rest comfortably on the certainty of God Himself. Her decision to submit stands upon the integrity of God's Word. Submission unto her husband will be the outgrowth of her commitment to her Heavenly Father's Word. In reality, a wife's decision to submit to her husband is essentially an issue that she decides between herself and her Heavenly Father. It is because she trusts God, and has confidence in what He asks her to do, that she will, deliberately and purposely, submit to her husband.

When a wife understands her God-given purpose in marriage she can move ahead and accomplish it. Because she knows and understands "the will of the Lord" she can give herself wholeheartedly to doing it. Again, her ministry of submission to her husband is based first and foremost upon her love and submission to the will of her Heavenly Father. Because of the love she has in her heart for God, she can love and honor her husband all the more. Submission to her husband will not be a heavy burden to be performed. There is no need for her to maintain a begrudging attitude or a spirit of resentment and rebellion. Married life for her can be peaceful and satisfying because she has learned to be a joyful giver to her husband. Submission from the heart will be a victorious lifestyle for her to enjoy. Jesus Christ said the following to his disciples about the importance of his work and the driving force that moved him to accomplish it.

John 4:34:
Jesus saith unto them, My meat [my food] is to do
the will of him that sent me, and to finish his work.

Jesus delighted to do the will of his Father. It was not always easy. Still, he rejoiced in pleasing his Father. A wife who is married to a Christian husband ought be real thankful for her man. When she finds submission to him to be like a pain-in-her-neck, maybe she could stop and think about Christian wives who are married to unbelieving men. Maybe she could stop and think what that must be like. And yet, God's Word to wives married to unbelieving men is that they are to be in subjection to them (I Peter 3:1-3). It is true that a wife will not always find submission to be a "bowl of cherries." There may be times when submission for her becomes as "hard as nails." There will be times when her husband's decisions seem ridiculous and out-of-bounds, and she may well know best about a particular decision, and be completely right about it. Even still, in these hard-time situations, she will need to submit to her husband. Why will she do it? That is how much she loves and trusts God!

Submission on the part of a Christian wife will, no doubt, set her apart from our modern-day culture. Her lifestyle will, most assuredly, be different from other wives she may know. She will have become the "radical" according to the accepted standard of the day. Her decision to submit to her husband will be out-of-step with what is practiced in the vast majority of marriages across this land. Nevertheless, submission to her husband remains her calling from on high. It is her rightful place in marriage. It is her God-given duty and she can rejoice in nothing less. Submission to her husband is the lifestyle in which she will find her greatest fulfillment. Any other disjointed marriage arrangement would absolutely be a compromise to the will of God. Role reversal marriages are misdirected, up-side-down arrangements, that foster misery and lead to divorce. Once a beautiful Christian wife has gotten to the place that, "thus saith the Lord," is the watchword in her life, there is no stopping her. Worldly marriage values become a secondary consideration to her. She knows that the standards of this temporal world are going to fade away. The driving motivation in her heart is to please God first.

Finally, the phrase "unto your own husbands," in our study of Ephesians 5:22, defines the sphere of a wife's submission duties. Here, her submission is in the context of her marriage relationship. She submits to no other man the way she does to her husband. No where in the Bible does God ever command a general submission of women unto men in society.

The phrase, "as unto the Lord," at the end of verse 22, defines the motive which leads her to submit unto her husband. It's because God has asked her to do so. She responds to what God has asked her to do. The same kind and quality of meekness that she shows to God, she is to bestow upon her husband's life. She does not worship her husband as God; rather, she honors her husband's authority to be her head in marriage. Because she respects her Heavenly Father, she submits to her husband. When she submits to her husband, she is indeed submitting to God's Word.

Christ and the church is the model after which the marriage relationship is built. Just as Jesus Christ took on the responsibility for the well being of his church, the husband is to take on the responsibility for his wife's well being.

Ephesians 5:23-24:
For the husband is the head of the wife, even as Christ is the head of the church: and he is the saviour of the body.
Therefore as the church is subject unto Christ, so let the wives be to their own husbands in every thing.

173

To be subject "in every thing" is a big expectation. In other words, subjection to a husband is not to be an "on-again, off-again" practice. There are a few exceptions that override "in every thing." If a husband requires his wife to do that which is unmistakably contrary to the Word of God he has lost his biblical authority and his wife must then obey the higher authority, she obeys God rather than her husband. This does not mean that she uses some flimsy, out of context, biblical excuse to justify her rebellion. When a woman disobeys her husband on the pretense that she is obeying only God, she is in reality disobeying God. Insanity would be a possible justification for her disobedience. She should not submit to physical violence or endangerment to her life and limb—this is inclusive of their children. She would certainly be justified in refusing to participate in the unnatural act of anal sex. The rectum is for waste removal, not for sexual intercourse. Adultery by her husband gives her a biblical justification to put him away by divorcement. However, the Bible does not teach that she <u>must</u> do so. She can forgive him when he becomes repentant. Then she would continue to obey him. The Church of Jesus Christ does not go around trying to "weasel out" of obedience to the Savior. The church strives to obey Jesus Christ in every thing, in every way. This is, of course, what the verse is talking about. A wife seeks to obey her husband in every way. She does not try to find some justification for her disobedience.

Even though a wife is asked to submit to her husband in every thing, in the very next verse (Ephesians 5:25) God tells the husband to love his wife even as Christ loved the church.

Marriage takes both parties fulfilling their duty. And, what a winning agenda this becomes. His deep-hearted love and her submissive spirit are the two essential qualities by which they can build a strong, binding marriage union. God has set it up so that a husband and wife are joined together by these two tremendous realities. When he loves, and she is obedient, they can rejoice in the companionship they share. Anything short of this is out-of-step with a godly union.

"AS IT IS FIT IN THE LORD"

The next reference that asks a wife to submit to her husband is found in the book of Colossians.

> **Colossians 3:17-18:**
> **And whatsoever ye do in word or deed, do all in the name of the Lord Jesus, giving thanks to God and the Father by him.**
> **Wives, submit yourselves unto your own husbands, as it is fit in the Lord.**

The context for the reference above is the disciplined walk of faithful Christian Believers. They are encouraged to live in the power of the spirit of God. They are to love the things that are "above" by keeping their minds on eternal values. They are to live by the power of the name of Jesus Christ in all that they say and do. They are to maintain thankful hearts unto their Heavenly Father. A Christian wife is to stay attuned to what God has established for her to do in marriage. This is not the first time, nor will it be the last, that God speaks frankly about the role of a wife. God has asked her to submit to her husband and she should be willing to do so. The motivation for her submissive spirit to her husband is reverence and respect for God. This is what God has asked of her—"as it is fit in the Lord."

When a godly wife submits to her husband, what a testimony her life becomes. She becomes a witness to the people of the world! This meek-hearted wife will have sanctified the Lord God in her heart, and she will be ready to give an answer to others concerning the "hope that lives within her." She will be seeking those things that are above, where Christ is seated on the right hand of God. Her affection will be on things above, as opposed to "worldly" values. A wife who has no problem with, "as it is fit in the Lord," is manifesting a beautiful spirit. Her beautiful spirit is akin to Mary's spirit of meekness when she said to the angel Gabriel, "Behold the handmaid of the Lord, be it unto me according to thy word"(Luke 1:38). Mary's meek, submissive heart to her Heavenly Father qualified her to give birth to the Savior of the world. "As it is fit in the Lord," conveys the same heart as, "be it unto me according to thy Word." A wife's meek, submissive heart to her husband is the means by which she can give birth to the heavenly marriage God has designed for her to enjoy.

WON BY THE BEHAVIOR OF THE WIVES

The next verses that ask a wife to submit to her husband are found in I Peter 3:1-6. Much can be gained here by looking at the overall context in which these verses are set. The words in this Epistle of I Peter are addressed to Judean

Christians who were scattered across Asia Minor. However, all who are born-again of God's spirit can profit from its message. The message of this Epistle calls our attention to some of the following:

- God has begotten us to a lively hope. He has given us a heritage that fades not away, it's reserved in heaven for us.
- We are kept by the power of God. For a season we are to patiently endure temptations and sufferings.
- We are to gird up the loins of our minds and be sober and hope to the end, to the appearing of Jesus Christ.
- We are to be done with our former lifestyle and live now as obedient children. We are to be holy in all manner of our living.
- We are to pass our sojourning here in reverence to God.
- We are to love one another with pure hearts, fervently.
- We are to maintain good works because they are a glory to God.
- We are not to render evil for evil, but rather we are to be a blessing to others.
- It's better that we suffer for the good we do, than to suffer for having done evil.
- Our former lifestyle was lived according to the "standards of the world." But, now we live by a <u>heavenly</u> standard.
- We are partakers of Christ sufferings, but when his glory shall appear, we will be glad with exceeding joy.

This is a little of the overall context in which wives are specifically asked to, "be in subjection to your own husbands." The testimony of a Christian wife will not go unnoticed. Yes, the high standard of a wife's Christian calling needs to be seen—it needs to be lived before the unsaved and dying. The marriage relationships of Christian wives are to become a living testimony to the great reality of the things of God—His presence and power, His peace and love, His mercy and forgiveness, His grace and goodness.

> **I Peter 3:1-4:**
> **Likewise, ye wives, be in subjection to your own husbands; that, if any obey not the word, they also may without the word be won by the conversation of the wives; While they behold your chaste conversation coupled with fear. Whose adorning let it not be that outward adorning of plaiting the hair, and of wearing of gold, or of putting on of apparel; But let it be the hidden man of the heart, in that which is not corruptible, even the ornament of a meek and quiet spirit, which is in the sight of God of great price.**

We need to closely observe the word "likewise." A better translation of this word would be, "in the same manner." This verse is asking wives to consider the examples of submission that have been given in the preceding chapter, and to behave "in the same manner" toward their husbands. In other words, they are asked to adapt their behavior so that it corresponds to the outstanding examples of submission that have been given to them already. These examples of submission are to become the pattern of behavior that wives are to follow. The first example they need to consider ask for Christian Believers to submit themselves to every ordinance of man for the sake of the Lord.

> *I Peter 2:13-15:*
> Submit yourselves to every ordinance of man for the Lord's sake: whether it be to the king, as supreme; or unto governors, as unto them that are sent by him for the punishment of evildoers, and for the praise of them that do well. For so is the will of God, that with well doing ye may put to silence the ignorance of foolish men.

The laws men make will not establish justice upon the face of the earth. Still, we graciously submit to their authority because God knows best, this is what He asks us to do. It is the will of God that by "well doing" (good works) foolish and ignorant men are going to be put to silence.

Wives are also to consider how Christian servants were asked to be submissive to their masters. These servants were encouraged to submit not only to good and gentle masters, but also to the harsh and overbearing. For them to do so would become a testimony of their obedience to God!

> *I Peter 2:18-20:*
> Servants, be subject to your masters with all fear [respect]; not only to the good and gentle, but also to the froward. For this is thankworthy, if a man for conscience toward God endure grief, suffering

wrongfully. For what glory is it, if, when ye be buf-
feted for your faults, ye shall take it patiently? But if,
when ye do well, and suffer for it, ye take it patiently,
this is acceptable with God.

Christian servants were called upon to patiently endure
having to suffer punishment even when it was unjust. Even
when they were punished after "having done well" still, in
reverence to God, they were to show patience toward their
unjust masters. They were called upon to live beyond the
normal standard of revenge. They were not to display an
eye-for-an-eye attitude when they were wronged. Their calling was to go beyond the "normal." They had been bought
with a price—they belonged to God. It's true that they were
the servants of men, but they were more than the servants
of men, they were first and foremost servants of God.

The life and ministry of Jesus Christ is the third example of
submission set before the eyes of Christian wives. His life of
steadfast obedience to God is the pattern of behavior wives
are to follow.

I Peter 2:21-25:
For even hereunto were ye called: because Christ
also suffered for us, leaving us an example, that ye
should follow his steps: who did no sin, neither was
guile found in his mouth: who, when he was reviled,
reviled not again; when he suffered, he threatened
not; but committed himself to him that judgeth
righteously: who his own self bare our sins in his
own body on the tree, that we, being dead to sins,

should live unto righteousness: by whose stripes ye were healed. For ye were as sheep going astray; but are now returned unto the Shepherd and Bishop of your souls.

It is by looking at these tremendous examples of submission that a wife understands why she is to submit to her husband. These examples answer both the why and how of submission. They make her rich in understanding because they teach her to compare the price of submission against the valuable return of pleasing her Heavenly Father, and the rewards that await her now and in eternity. They teach her to cleave to the Word of God in the face of difficult situations. They show her how to respond to injustice and harshness. They teach her to arm herself with the mind of Christ, and to offer up spiritual sacrifices to God. Debi Pearl's remarks on this subject are helpful.

A man will resist with all his might those who come against him. Most women spend their whole married lives in conflict with their husbands, trying to change them. It is a battle of the wills that no woman has ever rightly won, for even if she gets his compliance, she loses his heart, and he loses his self-respect. While we women tend to reduce everything to the issue of "who is right and what is just," God authoritatively points us to the real issue—"Whom did I place in charge, and whom did I create to be a help meet?" When a woman resists, or tries to change a man, she makes him more stubborn, and her own heart will be filled with bitterness. If a woman obeys God, a man does not have anything to come against, to resist, to dominate, to conquer, or to beat down. A woman's greatest power is in obeying God through obeying and honoring her husband. When she departs from God's order, she is setting herself up to create a life of turmoil, bitterness, and defeat—or both of them.[23]

I Peter 4:17 tells us the time has come that judgment must begin at the house of God. It certainly needs to begin at the house of God where the image of Christian marriage is concerned. Who can tell the difference between the marriages of Christians, and the marriages of unbelievers? What do the people of the world see about "Christian marriage" that is so different? It's very sad to say, but the truth is, very little difference can be seen between the two of them. If people are seeing squabbling; contention; unrest; hurt; infidelity; disdain; mocking; hatred; rejection; separation; and divorce in Christian marriages, they are seeing the ways of the world. They are seeing the "will of the Gentiles," so to speak. This desperately needs to change.

It is time for "judgment to begin at the house of God" where Christian marriages are concerned. What people need to see is a remarkable, outstanding difference between the marriages of Christian Believers and the marriages of unbelievers. Unbelievers need to think it strange that we are not running with them to the same excess of riot (I Peter 4:4). In other words, they need to see the outstanding beauty of a godly marriage. They need to see love and respect between a husband and wife. They need to see the godliness of a wife who respects and obeys the authority of her husband. They need to see a godly husband who loves and honors his wife. They need to see a husband and wife that are together "heirs of the grace of life" and are living the beauty and grace of their dynamic marriage union. This is the testimony that the dying, confused, people of the world need to see in a Christian marriage.

THE DYNAMIC INFLUENCE OF A RADIANT WIFE

The book of I Peter teaches how to live a godly life in the face of a godless world. This is what a Christian wife can and should do for an unbelieving husband. To lead a husband (or a wife) to God and see them born-again of His spirit is a tremendous accomplishment. What could be more important? This can certainly change a marriage and make it far better. This transformation might come to pass with just a few simple words that engender belief, or it could take years of faithful living to persuade an unbelieving mate. The godly conduct of a wife can make the difference for her unbelieving husband. He needs to see her "talking the talk, and walking the walk." When he observes behavior that exemplifies the power and loving grace of God in the way his wife lives, this is just what he needs to see. This is the kind of behavior that will influence anyone who can be persuaded.

The key verses we are studying (I Peter 3:2-4) encourage wives to live radiant lives before their husbands. The word "conversation" used here in the second verse is out of date, and it is better-translated "behavior." The chaste behavior of a wife can work wonders in the heart and mind of her mate. Her "high standard of morality" and her "spirit of respect" can become a powerful inspiration to her man. Her outward appearance is, generally, going to be a reflection of her inner beauty.

The way his wife presents herself to others is important to a husband. She can honor or dishonor her husband by the way she displays herself to others. Her wearing of flashy, provocative, clothing, ornate jewelry, or her showing lack of dignity, can be a big "turn-off" to him. Who is she trying to impress, anyway? Flashy, suggestive attire is often worn to call attention to one's sensuality. The way individuals choose to dress is usually a reflection of what is going on in their heads and hearts. Her sensuality is to be for her husband and why would she display it for the eyes of other men to see? A wife's restraint and modesty gratifies her husband. It takes her chaste behavior, the purity of her heart, to win his heart.

Proverbs 12:4:
A virtuous woman is a crown to her husband: but she that maketh ashamed is as rottenness in his bones.

When a wife behaves with a meek and quiet spirit towards her husband, how blessed he becomes—he is on top of the world! By living her life after this fashion a wife has also become a dynamic witness! Just to be in the presence of such a woman can be gratifying. Her life is not about the vanity of impressing people with her outward beauty and sexual charms. She is not "displaying herself" by dressing for an outward show. (There are plenty of wives around who dishonor their husbands by showing their sexual charms, and their promiscuity to on-lookers.) Rather, this wife stands before her Heavenly Father, her husband, and the people of this world, clothed in the righteousness of Jesus Christ. She exalts the Christ in her. Her adorning shines as a bright light in a world of darkness. Her meekness of spirit toward her husband is a light that shines before all those who see her marriage. The rich depth of her marriage relationship can teach others to trust God and to believe His Word. When an unbelieving husband, or the unbelieving people of this world, look upon this wife's meekness of heart, they should be drawn to the outstanding testimony of her life. The meek-of-heart will behold the testimony of her life and be lifted up by it. They will see that her life is a blessing, that she is a winner, and that she has nothing to fear. She's the godly, virtuous, wife any man would just love to have for his very own.

I Peter 3:5-6:
For after this manner in the old time the holy women also, who trusted in God, adorned themselves, being in subjection unto their own husbands: Even as Sara obeyed Abraham, calling him lord: whose daughters ye are, as long as ye do well, and are not afraid with any amazement.

A beautiful, meek and quiet spirit is truly a glorious thing to behold. The example of Sarah's kind, meek, spirit unto her husband, Abraham, sets a high standard. This beautiful woman was willing to literally put her life "on-the-line"

185

in support of her husband. In a special kindness to her husband, she agreed to support his request that in their travels, through dangerous lands she would say of him, "He is my brother." Abraham believed that ruthless pagans would kill him in order to take his beautiful wife. This kindness that he asked of her involved high stakes. She was willing to back-up her husband's "half truth" even to the Pharaoh (king) of Egypt. Her husband's plan almost led Sarah into an adulterous relationship with the Pharaoh. It took God's intervention to set things straight.

On another occasion in the land of the Philistines, Abraham informed Abimelech, King of Gerar, regarding Sarah, "She is my sister." So Abimelech sent and took Sarah from Abraham's camp. Here also, it took God's intervention to get Abraham and Sarah out of trouble. Of coarse, Sarah suffered shame and embarrassment, being reproved, while in the court of Abimelech. Because she had presented herself as a sister to Abraham, when the full truth came out, she was humiliated before the people of Abimelech's court. It required a lot for Sarah to stand by her man, but through thick-and-thin that is just what she did. What a giving, supportive, selfless, wife!

Sarah trusted her husband and dwelt confidently under the covering of his protection. Even in a godless land where powerful men took what they could by force, Sarah "stood by her man." God's promise to Sarah's husband was, "I will bless them that bless thee, and curse him that curseth thee: and in thee shall all families of the earth be blessed." (Genesis 12:3) Sarah believed in Abraham and she courageously supported her husband's calling. Abraham's God was also her God. She shared in that promise God made to her husband.

Sarah's courageous, obedient, support of her husband enabled her to travel by his side not knowing where they were going. And, though she bore the pain and disappointments of a barren wife for over seventy years of marriage, she faithfully submitted to her husband, calling him lord. Finally, she gave birth to a son when she was ninety years old. By believing God she (at the age of ninety) miraculously received strength to conceive and give birth. She was able to do so because, "she judged Him faithful who had promised" (Hebrews 11:11). What a wife! What an example! Her meek, quiet, spirit of submission to her Heavenly Father and to her husband, remains the example that calls out to wives everywhere today. This is how to do it! This is how to please your Heavenly Father. This is the way to please your husband. This is the way to witness to an unbelieving mate. This is the way to "Let your light so shine before men that they may see your good works and glorify your father which is in heaven" (Matthew 5:16).

To wear the ornament of a "meek and quiet spirit," a modern-day wife will need to lay aside her fears and restraints. She will need to wholeheartedly embrace the biblical directive for marriage. Fears will stifle and undermine her spirit of submission. She will need to go "full-guns-ahead" in trusting God. She must know, in her "heart of hearts", that God's hedge of protection is about her life. Just as God watched over Sarah's life, He in going to watch over her life also. She must be fully persuaded that the promises of God are going to come to pass for her personally—that God means what He has declared. She will need to reject the voices that call out for her to be her "own" woman. She will need to ignore belittling and scoffing from friends and acquaintances. Today, in our feministic culture, a God-fearing, God-trusting wife, who lovingly and joyfully submits to her husband, is almost like a "stranger and a pilgrim on the earth." However, just like Sarah received strength to conceive and deliver, a God-trusting wife will get the job done! God will gladly and abundantly strengthen her life and help her to stand. God will empower her life. He will provide the strength and guidance she needs day by day as she looks only to Him.

HOW TO BEHAVE IN THE HOUSE OF GOD

In I Peter 3:1-6, the focus was upon the witness a submissive wife could have to her unbelieving husband and to the "unsaved." The overall context for the Epistle of I Timothy has to do with how church leadership is to behave itself in the House of God. The next scripture we are going to look at focuses upon wives who were married to elders, bishops, and deacons in the church at Ephesus. Their behavior was "falling short," it was not setting a good example before the church fellowship.

> **I Timothy 2:9-12:**
> **In like manner also, that women adorn themselves in modest apparel, with shamefacedness and sobriety; not with broided hair, or gold, or pearls, or costly**

**array; But (which becometh women professing god-
liness) with good works.   Let the woman learn in
silence with all subjection.   But I suffer not a woman
to teach, nor to usurp authority over the man, but to
be in silence.**

The Church leaders at Ephesus were not the only ones with
wives who were out of order.   The Apostle Paul addressed
this same problem in his Epistle to the Corinthian church.

I Corinthians 14:34-36:
Let your women keep silence in the churches: for
it is not permitted unto them to speak; but they are
commanded to be under obedience, as also saith
the law.   And if they will learn any thing, let them ask
their husbands at home: for it is a shame for women
to speak in the church.   What? Came the word of
God out from you? or came it unto you only?

Wives, whose husbands were functioning in positions of
spiritual leadership, were out of order in both of these
church fellowships.   In the church at Ephesus, they were out
of order with the way they chose to dress themselves.   The
testimonies of these women were at stake.   Their husbands
were men of God, providing leadership to their church fellowships.   Their behavior, as <u>wives of church leaders</u>, should
have been exemplary.   However, the manner in which they
were dressing themselves was calling attention to their styl-
ish charms.   Braided hair and flashy apparel were fashion
statements that exemplified worldly values.   To be effective
witnesses of the Lord Jesus Christ they needed to adorn

themselves with modest apparel, modest behavior, and good works. A later reference describes how they were to function before the eyes of their church fellowships; "Even so must their wives be grave, not slanderers, sober, faithful in all things" (I Timothy 3:11).

In both churches, wives of church leaders were undermining the God-given authority of their husbands by voicing their opinions in the fellowship meetings as if they were the more qualified to speak. Their behavior was unbecoming. They should have honored their husbands. Their husbands were "men of God," who functioned with gift ministries, in service to their church fellowships. The statement above, "for it is a shame for women to speak in the church," points out the immodesty and offensive nature of their actions. They were trying to out-rank their husband's God-given authority. Their speaking out-of-turn was surely degrading to their husbands. They should have been setting an example by respecting their husbands and the ministries their husbands were performing for the church. This is why they were to "learn in silence." The Word of the Lord was coming "unto them," and unto God's people, by the ministries of their husbands. If these women needed some further instruction they were to stop interrupting their husbands and ask about it privately at home.

The essential work of a minister's wife is not the ministry of teaching the Word and proclaiming doctrines and precepts. Her ministry is the teaching that comes by the example of serving the needs of her husband. Certainly, she should learn the Word of the Lord, from the life of a godly husband who is teaching it to her. Her silence before the church will enable her to learn. It is her meekness of heart that will allow her to take it in. She is not to be so busy trying to run the show that she can not hear and see the valuable words and examples of godly living from her husband. Now, this may sound a little idealistic to some, but this is the quality of life that those who are serving God's people must live.

A word to a wise-hearted wife is in order here. Staying quiet on the inside and listening and learning from your husband is good advice for any wife. You need to give your husband the latitude that he needs to set the pace and to decide what's best—his leadership in the marriage is a big responsibility. He is responsible for himself but he is also responsible for you. Your confidence in his God-given authority is essential. There is no need for you to "butt-in" and try to take over responsibilities that do not belong to you. There is no need for you to take upon yourself needless cares, burdens and frustrations that he can handle far better. You do your job, and don't interfere with his. Offer your opinions and suggestions to him in an attitude of respect and reverence for his position of authority. Show meekness and deference to his leadership; don't try to take over and run the show. You are going to mess up your marriage big-time if you usurp his authority. If you have a tendency to do so, stop doing that right away. Let go, and let God. A stiff-necked, self-willed wife, who insists on running the show, is building a house that will not stand.

It is important to understand that these words, "let your women keep silence in the church," and "let the woman learn in silence," are addressed <u>only</u> to the wives of church leaders. They were not addressed to women in general. It would be a serious mistake to take words addressed to the wives of ministers and make them applicable to all other wives. Again, these verses are not addressing all the women of the churches. The wives of ministers are singled out because they bear a bigger responsibility. They are helpers and supporters of men called upon to minister to the body of Christ. She, herself, must be worthy of respect—temperance and self-control are essential qualities that she will need to exemplify. She cannot be caught up in the unwholesome practice of gossiping about this and that. Just like Sarah, she must be serious-minded about the importance of her husband's calling. She is to honor her husband's position of authority because she understands its importance. Her duty is to remain faithful and trustworthy in the unique responsibilities that come with being married to a minister of God's people. And yes, there is a difference between her and the other wives in their church fellowship.

The Word of God does not exclude women from participating actively in a church fellowship. They are to serve as helpers on the basis of what is needed. There are only a few isolated examples of women in leadership roles in the Bible. There are eight references to prophetess in the Bible (two of which appear to be self-appointed). Generally, only men occupied leadership roles in biblical times. But when men did not step-up, and provide the leadership required, God would empower a woman, as in the case of the Prophetess Deborah. She provided spiritual leadership to the House of Israel after the judge, Ehud, was dead. The apostle Paul commended a lady by the name of Phoebe to the Christian church in Rome. He asked those in the Roman church to assist her in whatever she needed. He described Phoebe as one who had helped many in her home church fellowship.

In modern day Christian fellowships women occupy many leadership roles. They serve as pastors, deacons, teachers and in many other capacities. Today, they are occupying positions that men almost exclusively occupied throughout biblical times. Perhaps the biggest reason for this change is the overall failure of men to provide authoritative, spiritual, leadership. Far too many men have squandered their spiritual privileges and duties and have not responded to the needs in their homes and church fellowships. Their failure to meet these needs has left leadership voids. Women have stepped in and are shouldering the duties and responsibilities that men should have been bearing all along. And who can condemn them for the good they are doing? If a man is not going to respond to God's calling, and a woman will, God will empower the woman to serve.

It is important to keep in mind that gift ministries to the church are God's option. He does the calling and the empowering. No one is to take that honor to himself or herself. A strong willed woman that has stepped in and presumptuously taken leadership control in her church, and home, troubles her own life, and also those around her. The biblical example in which men provide leadership in the church should be the practice today also. That would be best, that is what men need to be doing. They need to step forward, in answer to God's call, and serve as apostles, prophets, evangelists, pastors, and teachers. Maybe women would be relieved, even rejoice, to see their husbands "stepping up to the plate" of spiritual responsibility. They would dearly love to see their men respond to God's calling and provide spiritual leadership. They would like to see it both in their church fellowships, and in their homes.

GOD KNOWS BEST

Remember that we are still dealing with the overall context of how leadership is to behave in the church of God. We have seen how women, who are married to husbands that minister in the church, have a duty to set a good example before their fellowship. They are not to usurp their husband's authority. The following verses add weight to what has already been said. They substantiate the position of authority that God has placed upon husbands, and especially husbands, who are serving as ministers in a church fellowship.

> **I Timothy 2:13-15:**
> **For Adam was first formed, then Eve. And Adam was not deceived, but the woman being deceived was in the transgression. Notwithstanding she shall be saved in childbearing, if they continue in faith and charity and holiness with sobriety.**

Remember that it was God's decision to make Adam first; and then, from Adams's flesh, He formed Eve. This was the order God alone chose. He did not make a mistake in the order of His decision to form Adam first. Nor did He make a mistake in conferring the authority of leadership upon His man. Adam was not the first to be deceived; he was not deceived, it was Eve who was deceived. Why would any wife be in a rush to take over the leadership responsibilities that belong to her husband? Remember that it was Eve who first transgressed. How presumptuous Eve became; she thought she knew best, even better than God Himself. One might ask, where was Adam's leadership during this event? His leadership faltered when he willingly followed after Eve's transgression.

The serpent (Satan) in this Genesis account must have considered the woman more vulnerable than the man—he approached her rather than the man. Obviously, Eve was not discerning enough. She did not recognize the deception of her adversary and she mistakenly entertained what he had to say. Satan's subtlety tricked Eve into doubting the integrity of God's Word. Eve, presumptuously, changed what God had said. She added the words, "neither shall you touch it," to what was originally said regarding "not eating" the fruit in the midst of the garden.

Satan's logic was diametrically opposed to what God had said. God said, if you eat the fruit you are (surely) going to die. Satan said, if you eat the fruit you (surely) will not die. Eve succumbed to the logic the tempter laid before her. The allurement of personal gratification enticed Eve. She was lured by the temptation to become god-like, to be "all knowing." Eve was doubtless a gorgeous woman, but her prideful egotism got completely out of bounds and she succumbed to what was acceptable in her own eyes.

Genesis 3:6:
And when the woman saw that the tree was good for food, and that it was pleasant to the eyes, and a tree to be desired to make one wise, she took of the fruit thereof, and did eat, and gave also unto her husband with her; and he did eat.

The example used in I Timothy, regarding Eve's deception, is first and foremost a message for a wife. The message is: "Stay put on what God has to say, don't be so fast to rush in and take control." It just might be an inflated self-image that makes a wife think she is better qualified to take the responsibilities of leadership in her marriage. God never gave that responsibility to a wife. The best thing a wife can do when her husband falls short in his leadership role is to encourage him to be the man he ought to be.

Deceptive feminist doctrines will continue to float around in our midst. A Christian wife needs to be on guard. She must not be deceived into believing she is better qualified to take charge and provide marital leadership. She must not be beguiled into usurping the authority of her husband. The simplicity of God's Word is always the best thing to practice in a marriage. No wife of a minister, or any other wife for that matter, should ever be so full of herself that she thinks her opinion counts for more than God's Word. The ornament of a meek and quiet spirit toward God's Word will make her a winner in her marriage, and also in her Christian walk.

Isn't it great how God closes this section of scripture (verse 15 above) by pointing to Eve's recovery? Everyone knows about Eve's failure, but we need to also acknowledge the dynamic example of her faithfulness. Despite her transgression, Eve was still capable of giving birth to children whose prodigy, one day, would bring forth the birth of Jesus Christ. As she grew, Eve learned to trust God more. Early on, when she gave birth to Cain, she pridefully proclaimed, look at what "I" have done. Eve, mistakenly, thought she had given birth to the Promised One, the Redeemer—he was so wrong! However, by the time Eve gave birth to her third son, Seth, her meekness had grown—"For God, said she, hath appointed me another seed instead of Abel"(Genesis 4:25). By remaining faithful to God, and to each other, Eve and her husband could fulfill the promises God had made to them. Thusly, they needed to live lives of soberness and sanctification. They needed to love God and one another, and this is just what they did. She and Adam produced the prodigy that led to the birth of Jesus Christ, the savior of all who believe.

The context of this verse fits as a part and partial of the examples that God is using to instruct and fortify the behavior of wives in church fellowships. Our wonderful wives should be encouraged by the example of Eve's life. They can learn from her failure, but also by her example of faithfully trusting God. What a change of heart Eve had! She grew to believe in the "Word of the Lord." It was submission of heart, and faithful obedience to God, which caused her to triumph in her life. The example of Eve's life has been laid before the eyes of wives everywhere and for all time. She proved the pain and sorrow of unbelief, but she has also proved that loving and believing God bears good fruit.

Proving "the Word of the Lord," by meekness and submission, needs to become the agenda, the purpose, and the high expectation, for any modern-day Christian wife. The doubts, the fears, the unbelief, the prideful egotism, and whatever else might hinder her heart, must be put-down and laid to one side. The simplicity and beauty of trusting God and taking Him at His Word is her sure path-way to success. Following this path will enable her, as it enabled Eve. (Eve became the mother of us all.) There is no reason for a wife to fail as she clings to these verses we have studied. As she does so, her life will become a glorious testimony to the respect that she has for the position of her husband, and also, the respect that she has for her God and Father.

WHAT TO TEACH IN THE CHURCH

The next scripture we are going to study asked that the younger wives, in the church, be taught several things; one of which was obedience to their own husbands.

Titus 2:1-6:
But speak thou the things which become sound doctrine: That the aged men be sober, grave, temperate, sound in faith, in charity, in patience. The aged women likewise, that they be in behaviour as becometh holiness, not false accusers, not given to much

wine, teachers of good things; That they may teach the young women to be sober, to love their husbands, to love their children, To be discreet, chaste, keepers at home, good, obedient to their own husbands, that the word of God be not blasphemed. Young men likewise exhort to be sober minded.

The Apostle Paul left a young minister, named Titus, on the island of Crete to set-straight unbecoming behavior in their church fellowships. His work was to ordain ministers who could provide dynamic leadership. These ministers would need to reprove those in the church that contradicted God's Word. They would need to correct rebellious Believers that were known to be open liars. They would also have to reprove those who were teaching myths, and the commandments of men. Rebellious Christians in their fellowships were claiming that they knew God, but in works they were denying Him (Titus 2:16).

The reputation of the Christian community on the Isle of Crete was at stake. Their behavior needed improvement. They needed to exemplify the standard of God's Word in the way they lived life. So what we are looking at in the verses above is instruction to specific groups of people. This instruction concerned the way they were to behave themselves in their church fellowships and before the eyes of the public. The older men needed to follow the sound reasoning of God's Word. They needed to be sensible and self-controlled. They were to show soundness in the faith of Jesus Christ by manifesting love and patience in their dealings with others.

The word "likewise" in reference to the older women in the above verse means that they too were to behave in the same manner. They were to honor God by the witness of their demeanor—the high standard of their morality and their good works. They were not to speak falsely of others, nor were they to get out-of-bounds by drinking excessively. By being examples of that which is good, they became qualified to teach others in their fellowships. By putting on the standard of God's Word, they became qualified teachers of the younger women.

On a personal note, I would like to say that this is exactly what needs to occur in Christian fellowships across our nation and throughout the world. There needs to be an exacting difference in the behavior of undisciplined unbelievers, and that of men and women who have "named the name" of Jesus Christ. Born-again men and women need to walk in the power and efficacy of their calling. The witness of the Word of God is at stake. We cannot be a friend of the world and a friend of the Lord Jesus Christ. Just like the older Christian wives in the fellowship on Crete, older wives in our fellowships need to put on the mind of Christ and close out the flaky standards of society. They need to cling to that which is good and shun that which is evil. What the eyes of young women in Christian fellowships need to see is proof that biblical marriage works. They need to see shining examples of biblical truths in action. They need to see older women who are graciously submitting to their husbands and are blessed by doing so. This is what the eyes of younger women are searching to see.

A little of what was said earlier needs to be repeated. The generation of rebellious women, who burned their bras and condemned biblical marriage standards, are continuing their agenda to impose their will upon our culture. They have successively amassed the power of both public opinion, and political muscle. They are continuing to call to young women in this day. On February 26, 2013, the Public Broadcaster Service aired a three hour documentary by the title, "Makers: Women Who Make America." In this documentary feminists did their best to give the appearance of legitimacy. They proclaimed their own goodness and righteousness. Their presentation bragged and boasted about their supposed successes; however, they continued to call evil good and good evil. The purpose of their program seemed an effort to make new recruits and to keep their "loyals" motivated. And yes, they were definitely fortifying their work of programming young women. The lifestyles they are asking young women to adopt are vain, and devoid of sound judgment. Their lifestyles remain at cross-purposes with the Word of God.

None of us should lie down before the intentions of vicious deceivers who "swallow-up" young women by their deceptive teachings. The enemy's lies need to be confronted. Older Christian women need to become our first-line-of-offense. They need to expose the deceptive, pernicious, evils of a feminist culture that has blinded the eyes of today's generation. They need to speak out against feministic illusions of grandeur by faithfully acting upon the sound doctrines of biblical certainty. They need to become living epistles by personally practicing biblical marriage. Lastly, they need to speak out and teach what younger women desperately need to understand—God's Word can be trusted!

How many older wives practice biblical marriage standards before the eyes of younger wives in our churches, today? This is exactly what older Christian wives were encouraged to do on the Island of Crete. For those of you older wives who are courageous enough to do so today, praise God! Good for you! **You are setting the right example**. You are the living witness that younger women need to see. If the younger wives in your fellowship aren't living biblical standards in their marriages give them a gentle nudge and some loving, encouraging, correction. This is the very action that God's Word asks of older women. Boldly point them to the biblical standard—the Living Word of Truth. They should be blessed just to see the quality of your commitment to the responsibility God has given you.

Praise God, today there are increasing numbers of wives who are standing forth and courageously embracing what the Bible teaches about marriage. They have embraced biblical standards for their marriages, and they have become outstanding examples to younger women. Take a look at the following:

- Debi Pearl's tremendous book on marriage. Her God-inspired book, *Created to be His Help Meet*, is the fruition of her having practiced biblical marriage for over 30 years, and with great success.

- Glenda Hotton's little booklet, *Help! I Can't Submit To My Husband,* is very supportive of biblical marriage.
- Elizabeth Rice Handford's book, *Me? Obey Him?,* not only shows the responsibility of submission, but also shows the blessings, the joys, and the privileges that living a life according to God's plan brings.
- Darlene Schacht in, *The Good Wife's Guide,* encourages women to joyfully serve their families. She offers good reasons for achieving a well managed home, backed by scripture and gleaned from experience.
- The web site: www.Truewoman.com has a list of short videos featuring women sharing their victories and successes in biblical-oriented marriages.

There is much more that will be profitable to young women. They will need to take the time to search it out. Those whom have chosen to obey the Word of God in their marriages are not alone. They should take the time to seek out like-minded women that have embraced biblical standards in their marriages; encouraging each other. Maybe they can set up weekly get-together fellowships to support each other by sharing hearts.

Next, we are going to look at the character qualities older women in the church were to teach younger Christian women. The older women on Crete were given the responsible to continue the education of younger women. This is the way that sound judgments, precepts, and commandments, were to be set before younger Christian wives.

SOBER MINDED

"The Word of the Lord" needs to become wisdom and guidance for young Christian women. It is by the soundness of "this wisdom" that younger wives are able to sustain themselves in the midst of a crooked and perverse world. This is what is meant by training younger women to be sober. Sober mindedness is relying upon the sound council of God's Word.

Proverbs 31: 26:
She openeth her mouth with wisdom; and in her tongue is the law of kindness.

Proverbs 24:3-4:
Through wisdom is an house builded; and by understanding it is established: And by knowledge shall the chambers be filled with all precious and pleasant riches.

If young women are not taught the wisdom of God's Word, they are apt to adopt the wisdom of a dying world. Preparing them, helping them to become fully equipped, is a responsibility that remains in the hands of their older "sisters in the Lord."

TO LOVE HUSBANDS AND CHILDREN

The older wives were also to teach the younger women to love their husbands and their children. The best way to teach is by example. The older women would need to show love for their husbands, and children, to be effective teachers to the younger women. This is, after all, the method God Himself uses to teach us. We are taught of God to love one another (I Thessalonians 4:9). God demonstrated His love toward us while we were yet sinners. He required His only begotten son, Jesus Christ, to lay down his life, by the shedding of his blood, to cleanse us of our sins. The price that God was willing to pay on our behalf is so amazing! "For God so loved the world that he gave His only begotten son" (John 3:16).

The younger women on the island of Crete certainly needed to be taught how to love their husbands and their children. This is also what younger women need to be taught today. When younger women gaze upon the lives of older women they need to see them meeting the needs of their families. They need to see some sacrificial giving and serving. They need to look upon the patient endurance, respect and admiration older women show toward their husbands. Seeing the love and giving of older women, in action, will fortify the lives of younger women. The loving behavior of our older women will become the model, and the building blocks younger women will adopt and utilize in their homes and families. This is how it works! Just words alone, will fail to get the job done. Words and deeds must line-up. Hypocrisy will fail; it will not get the job done. The example of loving service, from the heart, is the requirement and it is indeed a powerful teacher.

DISCRETION

Even though wisdom and love are at the top of the behavior list, there are still other qualities of character that young women need to learn. They also need to learn the very important practice of discretion. The earlier they learn to make careful decisions the better. Prudent choices, about the way they behave themselves, need careful attention. They need to think seriously about their appearance and the impact it has on others. Young women should be taught to exercise godly restraint in the way they choose to dress. As we have already seen, this is an important consideration. The beauty of a woman is so persuasive to a man. Provocative sexuality can quickly draw a man's attention and lead him to lust. Jesus addressed this subject and warned men not to look upon a woman with lustful eyes. He stressed the importance that men exercise restraint and discipline regarding the attraction a woman may be to him. Young women should take their full measure of responsibly in this matter. The powerful attraction, of her beauty and sexuality, is not to be flaunted before the public's eyes.

We have already seen that the Bible speaks directly to wives in several places about the way they choose to adorn themselves, and it always encourages modesty. A fashion statement is usually a reflection of what a woman values in her heart. The way she chooses to dress herself is usually a reflection of her personality, and also of her intentions. A young woman is not to present herself as a "frisky chick" calling out to all the roosters in her circle of friends, "Look at me, how sexy and voluptuous I am." She may get a lot of attention by displaying her sexuality, but her behavior really highlights her misguided vanity. This is the kind of behavior that is practiced by natural-minded unbelievers. If her circle of friends dress like this, she need to find new friends.

Godly-modesty and good tastes are what people need to see in the life of a young Christian lady. She needs to maintain the demeanor that is becoming to a woman of God. She is, after all, an ambassador of the Lord Jesus Christ.

Proverbs 2:10-11:
When wisdom entereth into thine heart, and knowledge is pleasant unto thy soul; Discretion shall preserve thee, understanding shall keep thee:

CHASTE

The word chaste includes the idea of purity in ones behavior; however, as it is used here, it refers to a person's dedication or consecration. In other words, the reason for ones purity of behavior is the result of his or her dedication to the things of God. The first one a young Christian woman needs to please is her Heavenly Father. God's Word teaches her the good, the bad, and the ugly. So, she needs to choose to do what God asks of her. She shows the love and dedication she has for her Heavenly Father by the way she lives her life before others. The way she lives her life sends a big message to those who are looking upon her. By her actions she is saying to those about her, "I am pleasing my God, and this is <u>why</u> I live the way I do. This is <u>why</u> I make the choices I make. I'm pleasing God, because He is the rewarder of those who diligently seek to please Him." Praise God! What an outstanding testimony she has! This young woman has left off the baggage of worldly values. She has put away the lust of the flesh, and the lust of the eyes, and the pride of life (I John 2:15).

Jesus Christ set the example of chaste behavior. He did not please himself; he dedicated his life to pleasing his Father.

John 9:4-5:
I must work the works of him that sent me, while it is day: the night cometh, when no man can work. As long as I am in the world, I am the light of the world.

Take a good look at what this earned him. He is seated at the right hand of God! Let me encourage you young ladies. Why not show the people of this world your brand of chaste behavior—your dedication to your Heavenly Father? Why not show them who you are? You are a young woman born-again of God' spirit. God has given to you the power and authority to walk before the people of this world clothed in the righteousness of Jesus Christ. You are a light in this world of darkness. You, just like your savior, must be about your Father's business. Living your life in dedication to God will make you a "radical" in the eyes of others, but this is your calling. You are living for higher stakes than the trinkets of this world. Your aim is to please God!

KEEPERS AT HOME

The verse we are studying (Titus 2:5) asks the older women to teach the younger women to be keepers at home. Nowhere in the Bible are men instructed to be keepers of the home. The outstanding assumption is that women are better qualified to take on this tremendous task. When it comes to the division of responsibilities in a marriage union it certainly makes sense that each one should assume the responsibilities they are best suited to handle. To be a "keeper of the home" involves a lot; it entails major responsibilities. Our homes, and families, remain the springboard from which other endeavors must emanate. The workplace provides financing for the home; however, our home life prepares us to meet the world.

I would like to share with you my personal expectation regarding my home life. I enjoy sitting on comfortable chairs and sleeping on a comfortable bed. I like nice surroundings in my home; cleanliness is important, order and decency are paramount. I enjoy thoughtful decorations and uplifting wall hangings. A peaceful, restful, environment is a big plus. I enjoy extending hospitality to others in my home, so a well kept home is necessary in order to do this. It is certainly nice to have scheduled meals, and good cooking. My wife and I raised a son and a daughter in our home. Their well being and training remained uppermost in our hearts because we wanted the very best for them. For me, a home needs to be a restful sanctuary of love, peace, and order.

When I met my wife, Carol, she practiced optometry and I'm sure she was very good at it. I personally did not care to be married to a professional woman. To have my wife close by, taking care of the important work of managing our home, was high on my priority list. I needed a wife by my side, being my helper. Carol cared for me enough to put her optometry profession to one side and take on a new career. She became Mrs. Charlie P. Johnston in April of 1979, and she has been the keeper of our home throughout the years of our marriage. This has been her "career" now for thirty-four years. Her beautiful heart of giving and serving is an inspiration to my life. Her faithfulness and loyalty are so outstanding. She is my friend, my helper, and my lover.

My wife's mother told me at our wedding, "I don't know what you two are going to do, Carol can't cook." Now, she may be the best cook in the county. She serves delicious meals. She has given herself to the task and the duties of keeping our home and being a tremendous helper to me, her husband. Oh, how she blesses my life! How thankful I am for her gracious, loving heart. She's much more than a stay-at-home mom. Her heart is to make our home a beautiful, comfortable, restful dwelling place. And she has given herself wholeheartedly to the work of guiding our home. She taught our children how to love and serve God by her words and by her deeds. She has kept our home free from the smut of this world and made it a beautiful dwelling place. She does all of this with a joyful heart and pride in her workmanship. She is a keeper of our home *par excellence.* Her dedication to our marriage is an outstanding example for any young wife who cares to learn, from her commitment, to do it God's way.

When a young woman chooses marriage, her marriage must become her highest priority. It is not a part time job. It should become her "career" and she would do well to think of it in this way. It's true that needs in marriages vary a great deal because we are all individuals. However, the establishing of a home will require certain fundamental assets and standards. A young Christian wife getting started in her marriage needs the right model. The model of God's Word asks a wife to guide the home because she is best suited for that responsibility. She alone bears the responsibility of birthing a child, and it is her duty to mother her child. She is to teach and train that child the truth of God's Word. She has sworn before God to be a companion and a helper to her husband. The focus in her life must now turn to ministering to her husband and their children. The home is the best possible place for her to meet the needs of her family. There are going to be plenty of needs to be met. Her time and attention in putting her home together, so that it functions at its best, will require her best effort. When a wife invests her energies into building her home and family, she can look forward to receiving big dividends.

A wife cannot sit around idly talking to girlfriends on the phone for hours and get her work done. It is so easy to become distracted by other things. It takes a concerted effort to be a good homemaker. If she is not there in the home she cannot be a successful "keeper of the home." Though it might become necessary in some situations, working outside of the home is usually second best. It can be a serious hindrance to home life. The right spirit and attitude will enable a young wife to be a successful keeper of her home. The duties and responsibilities of caring for her family are clearly defined for her by the "Word of the Lord." By keeping her head and heart focused on her husband, and children, she can provide the restful, up-lifting, home life her family needs. What a blessing she will be by having done so!

GOOD

Some commentators attach the word "good" in Titus 2:5 to being keepers at home. In other words: good at keeping the home. Others allow this word to stand-alone independently, and treat it on its own merit. It is certainly true that young wives should be taught to be good and kind. *Bullinger's Critical Lexicon of the Greek New Testament,* defines the meaning of "good," as it is used here, to be that which is to advantage another. In other words, "to be a blessing." So, we are able to see that "good" is associated with teaching the younger wives to be obedient to their own husbands. For indeed, if a young wife is willing to obey her husband that will be a good gift to him. Her obedience will be a blessing of goodness, or kindness, bestowed upon her husband's life.

OBEDIENT TO THEIR OWN HUSBANDS

The older women in Crete were not dealing with the onslaught of a feminist movement; however, the "obedient to husbands lesson" was an essential teaching for their younger women. The Greek word *hupotasso* is translated "obedient" here in Titus 2:5. However, it is the same Greek word that is translated submission or subjection in other places. The emphasis here in Titus is upon what younger women are to be taught. The biblical message, concerning the proper role of a wife, is absolutely clear. Over and over again, God has asked wives to honor the authority He has given to husbands. This is clearly God's plan. Submission, obedience, and subjection are words mocked by women-liberation sympathizers. Consequently, these words may have an unpleasant connotation, even for some Christian women. It should be helpful for those who are continuing to wrestle with these biblical directives to keep their focus in the right place. The bottom-line meaning of submit, obey, and subject, asks a wife to willingly place herself under the God-given authority of her husband by following his leadership and carrying out what he asks of her. This is her kindness to him. And, she behaves in this manner because her first duty is to please her Heavenly Father.

For an entire generation now, the Christian community, as a whole, has failed to teach young women to obey their husbands. The biblical curriculum of marriage has gathered dust. God's Word has not remained the source book used to guide the thinking of young women. This is one major reason why marriage failures are so commonplace. Young couples are making up their own rules of engagement and why should we be surprised? The Christian community has not risen up to stand in opposition to the dismantling of biblical marriage. That is why thousands upon thousands of young men and women are choosing to live together outside of wedlock.

There is, of course, no reason to believe that this will change if Christians continue to keep their mouths closed in silence. The need to speak out is urgent. This is the hour for Christian Believing men and women, husbands and wives, old and young, to brush-off the dust from what God's Word declares about Christian marriage. We need to repent of our laxity and our silence. Complacency, with the way things are, guarantees that nothing will change. The way things are headed now, the devastation of divorce, and the consequences of fornication, will continue to shatter the lives of our sons and daughters. God-ordained marriage will continue to be mocked and belittled, as it is today. The Christian community needs to rise up and stand against the onslaught of those who are seeking to undermine marriage and family life.

The first thing that needs to occur is for those in church leadership to own up to their failures. They have failed to teach what needs to be said regarding biblical marriage. They have bowed to the fierceness of the enemy and allowed their people to be taken captive by devilish doctrines. Pastors, and church leadership, need to step forward and lead the way. They need to honor their calling and get with the accuracy of what the Bible teaches regarding marriage. They need to take their stand upon the truth and accuracy of the Bible and let the chips fall where they may. Who are they trying to please, anyway? They need to please God who called them to stand in the gap and to warn God's people about the devices of the devil. It is time for them to rise up with strength of will, and strength of purpose, and fully teach biblical marriage—no reserves, no caution, full speed ahead, damn the torpedoes!

All of us need to wake up and recognize the impending danger. The way we are headed we are in jeopardy of loosing the fundamental meaning of marriage. The enemy is playing for keeps! One day you might be really shaken to discover that your son or daughter has chosen to "shack up" with a mate. What a tragedy that would be for you, and for them. There is simply no place for timidity or cowardice in the hearts of men and women born-again of God's spirit. Sin is wrong, it must be confronted. The light of God's Word dispels darkness. To compromise truth fosters evil. The error of a generation of silence must come to an end. It's time to get vocal with our words and our deeds. This is the need and this is the agenda to which we must respond. We must stand firmly on the living "Word of the Lord" regarding biblical marriage and fight tenaciously for the lives of our sons and daughters. Marriage God's way is exactly what we must teach our young women and men. We need to prove it in our lives personally, and we need to speak it to a confused world, headed for destruction. Look at what our silence has gotten us. It has fortified the enemy. What do we have to fear? God will take care of His people. He will stand beside those who choose to speak on His behalf.

I John 4:4:
Ye are of God, little children, and have overcome them: because greater is he that is in you, than he that is in the world.

THE RIGHT TESTIMONY

The concluding words of Titus 2:5 are, "that the word of God be not blasphemed." A better translation of this phrase is: so that no one can reproach the Word of God.[24] When our behavior lines up with the Word of God we have a strong testimony for the eyes of others to gaze upon. On the other hand, when we claim to be men and women of

God but our behavior does not exemplify God's Word, we have a problem. The eyes that gaze upon us see a contradiction between what we say and what we do. In fact, when this is the case, we have become hypocrites to those that look upon our lives. Behaving in this manner is a reproach to the Word of God—we will have discredited it. Rather than being a guiding light, our behavior becomes a stumbling block.

When the young women on the island of Crete were displaying modesty, loving their husbands and their children, discreet in their behavior, chaste (dedicated to the things of God), being good home makers, and obeying their husbands, they were pleasing God. Their behavior exemplified the grace and beauty of their Christian calling. When they were living this way, their lives became a manifestation of the power and presence of God in Christ in them. Their lives became a living testimony to the truth of God's Word. This is the way young women need to live today. This is how they will please God! This is how they will show forth the Excellency of God's praise. They will have ceased their friendship with the world, but the glory of their lives will be an outstanding testimony to the reality of their new birth. They are born-again of God's spirit, and the entire world can see it.

SOME CONCLUDING REMARKS

All of the six sections of Scripture we have studied ask a wife to submit to her husband. Each of them deals with specific aspects and purposes for her submission. Collectively, they teach the fullness of what a wife needs to understand about submission to her husband. They provide a wife so much of the necessary information she needs to be her best in marriage.

The next thing we are going to do is to draw a few conclusions from this study. The following is a short review of some of the essential things we have learned:

In Ephesians 5:21-22, we learned that obedience from the heart is on a higher plane than obedience that is required. Obedience to the Word of God from the submissive heart of a wife is the fundamental key to her having a great marriage. All authority belongs to God. When a wife acknowledges that the "Word of the Lord" has established her husband's leadership position of authority her believing can rest on the certainty of God Himself.

In Ephesians 5:23-24, we learned for a wife to be subject in everything is a big expectation. However, she should always seek to obey her husband. She does not go around trying to find some justification for her failure to obey him. She is to seek to obey her husband in the same way the church strives to obey Jesus Christ.

In Colossians 3:17-18, we learned a Christian wife is to stay "keyed into" what God established for her in marriage. God has asked her to submit to her husband and she should be willing to do so. The wife who has no problem with "submit yourselves unto your own husbands as it is fit in the Lord" will be pleasing her Heavenly Father. She will be manifesting the same beautiful spirit seen in Mary's life when she said to the angel Gabriel, "Behold the handmaid of the Lord, be it unto me according to thy word." A wife's meek and submissive heart to her husband is the means by which she can give birth to the heavenly marriage God has designed for her to enjoy.

In I Peter 3:1-4, we looked at the three outstanding examples of submission that were set before the eyes of a Christian wife. She was asked to pattern her submission to her husband after these examples. The first example was "submit yourselves to every ordinance of man for the Lord's sake." The second example was that of Christian slaves being obedient to their masters, not only to the good and gentle, but also to those who were harsh. The third example was of Jesus Christ: who did no sin, who had no guile in his mouth, who when he was spoken evil of he spoke not evil again, and when he suffered he threatened not. In all of this, he committed himself to God. These examples teach a wife to compare the price of submission against the valuable return of pleasing her Heavenly Father. They show her how to respond to injustice and harshness. They teach her to arm herself with the mind of Christ. We also learned here that when a wife behaves with a meek and quiet spirit towards her husband her life becomes a dynamic witness. When the unbelieving people of this world look upon her meekness-of-heart they will be drawn to the outstanding testimony of her life.

In I Timothy 2:9-15, we learned that wives whose husbands were leaders in the church had special responsibilities.

They were not to undermine the God-given authority of their husbands by voicing their opinions in the fellowship as if they were more qualified to teach. They should have been setting an example by respecting their husbands and the ministries their husbands were performing for the church. The essential work of a minister's wife is not the ministry of teaching the Word and proclaiming doctrines and precepts. Her ministry is the teaching that comes by the example of serving the needs of her husband. Her confidence in her husband's God-given authority is essential.

We also learned that the words, "let your women keep silence in the church," are addressed <u>only</u> to the wives of church leaders. They are not addressed to women in general. The wives of ministers are singled out because they bear a bigger responsibility—they are helpers and supporters of men called upon to minister to the body of Christ. The Word of God does not exclude women from participating actively in a church fellowship. In biblical times when men failed to take leadership responsibilities God would empower a woman, as in the case of the prophetess Deborah.

If a man is not going to respond to God's calling, and a woman will, God will empower the woman to serve. Men need to rise up and be the first to respond to the "calling" of leadership in the church.

We also looked at the biblical example of how Eve was beguiled by the devil. We considered how many wives are still being beguiled into usurping the God-given authority of their husbands by taking control of the leadership role in their marriages. When they do so, they have rebelled against the Word of the Lord. They have been deceived into believing they are better qualified to take charge. Each and every wife must decide which word will stand. Is it her word and her opinion that is the authority in her marriage; or will she honor the word of her husband?

In Titus 2:1-6, we learned that just like the older Christian wives on the Island of Crete, older wives in our fellowships need to put on the mind of Christ and close out the flaky standards of society. God has given older wives the responsibility to teach the younger women and this is what they need to do. This responsibility has not changed. But now, for an entire generation, older women have failed to teach young women to embrace biblical marriage. Consequently, God's Word is not the source book that guides their thinking. But, complacency guarantees nothing will change. We need to repent of our laxity and our silence. This is an hour of need. The need is that we rise up and stand against the onslaughts of those who are seeking to undermine marriage and family life.

Marriage God's way is exactly what we must teach our young women and men. We need to prove it in our lives personally, and we need to speak it to a confused dying world. When our behavior lines up with the Word of God we have a strong testimony for the eyes of others to gaze upon. When our young women are displaying modesty, loving their husbands and their children, when they are discreet and chaste in their behavior, being good homemakers, and obeying their husbands, they exemplify the beauty and grace of their Christian calling. Their lives become a manifestation of the power and presence of God in Christ in them. Their lives then become a living testimony to the truth of God's Word.

Finally, before we close this study on submission, there is one last Scripture that we need to consider. It asks a wife to reverence her husband.

Ephesians 5:33:
Nevertheless let every one of you in particular so love his wife even as himself; and the wife see that she reverence her husband.

Ephesians 5:33 is actually the concluding remarks to the outstanding teaching that ask a husband and wife to pattern their behavior after their Savior. The relationship Christ shares with the church is the example they are to follow. Jesus Christ emptied himself in selfless giving. He always did the will of his Father. He was always obedient to the Word of God. He kept the first and great commandment in the law. He loved God with all his heart, and with all his soul, and with all his mind. He also loved his neighbor as himself (Matthew 22:37-39). The closer a husband's and wife's behavior gets to the standard of Jesus Christ's life of giving service, the better marriage they will enjoy. When a husband gets to the place that he can empty himself, of himself, and place the needs of his wife above his own, he is loving like his Savior loved. When a wife lovingly obeys her husband, even when the going gets really tough, she is loving and obeying like her Savior loved and obeyed.

A wife's duty in the marriage relationship is to show deference to her husband. She is asked to render the respect he is due. The Bible teaches us to render to all their dues; fear to whom fear, and honor to whom honor (Romans 13:7). The word fear used here is talking about respect—respect to whom respect is due. A duty is what one ought to do. A fundamental tenant of marriage, in the Bible, is that a wife ought to respect her husband. According to the Word of God, this is her duty, and no other options are given. The phrase "and the wife see that she," is asking for a wife to make a willful decision to fulfill her duty and to respect her husband. Just like she needs his love, he "needs" her respect.

The word "reverence" at the end of Ephesians 5:33 does not mean to venerate or to regard as sacred. But, it does mean to hold in high regard—to show feelings of deep respect. A wife's respect will certainly include an acknowledgment of her husband's God-given authority to lead their lives. The respect a wife has for her husband can express itself in many ways. The Amplified Bible's translation for this verse shows a few of these.

Ephesians 5:33b:
And let the wife see that she respects and reverences her husband [that she notices him, regards him, honors him, prefers him, venerates [[highly regards]], and esteems him; and that she defers to him, praises him, and loves and admires him exceedingly].

Now if this seems too much to ask of a wife, it certainly is not! This is exactly the way she should behave in marriage.

This behavior is the high calling of a Christian wife. It is asking no more of a wife to reverence her husband, after this fashion, than to ask a husband to love his wife after the pattern of the love of Jesus Christ. God shows no partiality. His marriage plan unites them in such a way that both partners become winners. This is easy to understand. When a wife respects her mate in this way, and a husband loves his wife in this manner, nothing is going to tear them apart—they will have become one flesh. There is no division between them. The squabbling and contention is over. There is unity in the abiding love they share between them. Their focus is in the right place. They are a huge blessing to each other. They are richly fulfilling each other's needs.

A little note to husbands is in order here. We husbands need to take special care to encourage our wives. We especially need to recognize the uphill battle our wives endure living in a feminist-dominated-society. They face tremendous pressure from multiple segments of American culture that asks them to fall in line and behave as other, so-called "liberated wives" are behaving. As a matter of fact, they have already observed that the vast numbers of women, in this day, do not submit to their husbands. Some of their closest friends may not submit to their husbands. Our wives need all the encouragement they can garner! We need to affirm the tremendous value of their position in our homes and the essential work that they perform for our benefit. We need to recognize their successes and praise them for their accomplishments. We need to let them know that we back them up in what they are endeavoring to do.

We need to let our wives know that we understand that they are in a battle that involves more than flesh and blood. Their decision to be an obedient wife is indeed a spiritual decision. They are in the midst of a spiritual battle, whereby the god of this world (the devil) is seeking to rob them of the joy that comes from fulfilling their God-appointed role in marriage. Our comforting words, and our prayers, will bring encouragement to their efforts. The spiritual leadership we husbands manifest in the presence of our wives, day-by-day, will also encourage them. They can enjoy real success in their decision to submit, because they are women born-again of God's spirit—they are empowered by the Spirit of God. He is going to help them. They can do it!

Ephesians 3:14-21:
For this cause I bow my knees unto the Father of our Lord Jesus Christ, of whom the whole family in heaven and earth is named, that he would grant you, according to the riches of his glory, to be strengthened with might by his Spirit in the inner man; That Christ may dwell in your hearts by faith; that ye, being rooted and grounded in love, may be able to comprehend with all saints what is the breadth, and length, and depth, and height; And to know the love of Christ, which passeth knowledge, that ye might be filled with all the fulness of God. Now unto him that is able to do exceeding abundantly above all that we ask or think, according to the power that worketh in us, unto him be glory in the church by Christ Jesus throughout all ages, world without end. Amen

CHAPTER 6

DIVORCE IN THE
BIBLE

⟨∾⟩

The purpose of this chapter is not to condemn those who have divorced. Praise God, His marvelous grace is greater than all our sins. The shed blood of Jesus Christ cleanses every Christian Believer's sins. "If we confess our sins, He is faithful and just to forgive us our sins, and to cleanse us from all unrighteousness" (I John 1:9). The goal is not condemnation. The goal here is to set the high standard of God's Matchless Word before us, and to cleave to that Word. We are obligated to live only by the high standard of God's Word; there is not a higher authority to guide us.

THE FAILURE OF CHRISTIAN MARRIAGE

Wedlock is a descriptive term sometimes used to describe marriage. It's a good term! The problem we have today is that disgruntled and unhappy couples are too quick to reach for the key and unlock a union God intended to last a lifetime. Blatantly ignoring God's Word in this matter is a huge mistake. The seriousness of this problem must be addressed. Divorce is a worldly, man-made, mechanism for dissolving a marriage. The need is that divorce remains outside the ranks of the Christian Community except in accordance with what is declared by the Word of God. There are far-reaching implications at stake when Christian couples divorce for non-biblical reasons.

It is plainly evident, ever increasing numbers of Christian homes and families are being torn apart because husbands and wives refuse to live together peacefully. Tens of thousands of them have divorced. The failure of Christian marriage is a "blight" upon the testimony of the Gospel of the Lord Jesus Christ. Most of these departing couples have failed to abide by their covenant promises and by doing so they have ignored the biblical standards they professed. The negative influence of these marriage failures continues to reverberate far beyond the divorcees themselves. The larger influence of Christians divorcing is casting doubts upon the intrinsic value of marriage itself. If Christians can't get it right, who can?

No one would seriously argue with the fact that our culture has revolted against the Most High. That surprises no one! However, it certainly is surprising to see that the Christian Community is ignoring the high calling of biblical matrimony. A thick layer of dust has settled upon the pages of the biblical instructions that husbands and wives should be personally putting into practice. But what they are actually practicing in their marriages is more akin to the marriage practices of God-rejecting, natural-minded married couples. Consequently, Christian marriage (as a whole) is failing to prove the standard it proclaims. Dust covered Bibles and God-rejection surrounding the unique relationship of Christian marriage just will not work!

The testimony of a hypocrite counts for nothing. When there is barely an "ounce of difference" between the conduct of Christian couples and that of non-Christian couples the power of God's Word has been mocked. And, what a problem this has become. This is a major reason that matrimony is being dismantled before our eyes. The hypocrisy of so called "Christian marriage" is in plain view, and everyone beholds it. In the eyes of the public, defunct Christian marriage is fully evident. It is the falling apart of Christian marriages that undermines the meaning of what marriage is supposed to be. Christian marriage is to be practiced according to the Living Word of God. The alarming consequence of "busted unions" is that God's marriage plan is belittled. If Christian husbands and wives are not willing to abide by the "Word of the Lord" the example of what marriage is supposed to be has been all together lost. And, today it is certainly lost! This is the reason that people have turned away from it.

High sounding platitudes about Christian marriage need the reality of flesh and blood, living action. The general public needs to "see a sermon." They have "heard a sermon," but they need to see a sermon. Until they "see the sermon" they will remain skeptical about what they have heard. They will cast it to one side, and in essence, this is what they have done. Even within the ranks of the Christian Community many young adults have abandoned the union of marriage. They are "shacking up" and living together outside of a marriage commitment. There seems to be little resistance to these "unwholesome arrangements" among the membership of church-going people. They are sitting idly by with "buttoned lips," and are accepting open fornication among their ranks—what is more troubling; they are exhibiting very little shame and remorse for having done so. Where is their out-cry?

This empty void between what is being said and what is being done by Christian husbands and wives must be filled. The high standard of Christian marriage must be proved by the example of Christian husbands and wives living together in peaceful harmony. Nothing succeeds like success. When Christian couples are practicing biblical marriage their presence gives off a warm glow. It is encouraging just to be around them. The beauty of their healthy marriage is in plain view. They become an inspiration to many. They are indeed a dynamic "duo." Others look upon their lives and say within themselves, "Yes, this is just what I would love to have in my marriage." A simple reality about life is that flies are drawn to honey. It's hard to keep them away. The impending need is that the Christian Community "puts the honey" back into their marriages. When Christian husbands and wives are practicing biblical marriage the testimony of their union proclaims the integrity of what God has established. The witness of their marriage becomes proof that God's Word is true. This is what people desperately need to see!

GOD'S PERSPECTIVE OF DIVORCE IS CLEAR

Malachi 2:16:
For the Lord, the God of Israel, saith that he hateth
putting away: for one covereth violence with his gar-
ment, saith the Lord of hosts: therefore take heed to
your spirit, that ye deal not treacherously.

God does not hate people. He does not hate in the sense
of human hatred. But He does oppose putting away a
marriage by divorce. The word "violence" in verse 16, is a
descriptive term that means to "snatch away or to tear apart."
Divorce tears apart the union of one flesh. It divides what
God has joined together. (What therefore God hath joined
together, let not man put asunder, Matthew 19:6.) Divorce
is more than physical separation. It is also the ripping apart
of two human spirits. It tears apart the mental stability of
one-minded togetherness. Divorce, almost always, destroys
emotional commitments—it produces loneliness and can
distort meaning and purpose in one's life. It can, and often
does, put a dampening effect on a Christian's testimony.
Its horrific effects are devastating. It is no wonder God
opposes it.

In the above verse, the phrase, "that ye deal not treacherously," is referring to the betrayal of a trust. In this passage, husbands had promised, by a covenant, to provide
companionship to their wives for the rest of their days.
However, their promises were deceitful. As we have already
seen, their words were meaningless. Instead of standing
by what they had coveted to do, they were divorcing their

wives. God challenged them to take heed to their spirit. He wanted them to perform what they had promised by an oath in His presence. This is also exactly what God expects of a husband and wife today.

Since it is God that unites a couple in marriage, it will never be a couple's option to determine what are legitimate grounds for a divorce. God set the terms for marriage and He alone sets the terms for divorce. When a married couple is out of fellowship with each other they are usually out of fellowship with their Heavenly Father. In one way or another, divorce is a result of sin. So, sinful divorce is an impediment to fellowship with God and needs to be corrected by restoration of the broken marriage union. The sticky mess of divorce can become so complicated that restoration seems impossible. But, the far-reaching consequences of divorce can stay with the departing couple for the rest of their days upon this earth. Their divorce will, almost always, work hardship and suffering upon themselves, their children, their families, and their friends. It is the standard of what the Word of God says that we must practice here in this matter. The Bible does allow for divorce under certain circumstances— those that God has determined. We need to recognize that divorce outside of these circumstances is sin and needs to be reckoned with as such.

OLD TESTAMENT TEACHINGS

Before the Law of Moses, Israelite women were without marital rights. Oral traditions were the law Israelites observed. An Israelite husband had to pay a dowry for his wife. Remember how Jacob worked for seven years to pay for Rachel? He didn't have money in his pockets for payment, so his labor paid for her. In that day, a wife was basically owned much like property. If a man chose to get rid of a wife, he thought it was his business, and he did so with few or no repercussions. In those days, husbands were abusing their wives by divorcing them, and sending them away for any reason they chose. This was the context in which the law regulating divorce was given. God's original marriage plan made no provision for putting away a wife; He declared that marriage is to last for a lifetime. To set the framework here, we need to look at the Old Testament laws that regulated divorce. God gave certain instructions to Moses that would curtail husbands from divorcing their wives and sending them away without any explanation. The first one deals with unscrupulous men who might seek to put away their bride by false accusations concerning her virginity.

Deuteronomy 22:13-21:
If any man take a wife, and go in unto her, and hate her, And give occasions of speech against her, and bring up an evil name upon her, and say, I took this woman, and when I came to her, I found her not a maid: Then shall the father of the damsel, and her mother, take and bring forth the tokens of the damsel's virginity unto the elders of the city in the gate: And the damsel's father shall say unto the elders, I gave my daughter unto this man to wife, and he hateth her; And, lo, he hath given occasions of speech against her, saying, I found not thy daughter a maid; and yet these are the tokens of my daughter's

virginity. And they shall spread the cloth before the elders of the city. And the elders of that city shall take that man and chastise him; And they shall amerce him in an hundred shekels of silver, and give them unto the father of the damsel, because he hath brought up an evil name upon a virgin of Israel: and she shall be his wife; he may not put her away all his days. But if this thing be true, and the tokens of virginity be not found for the damsel: Then they shall bring out the damsel to the door of her father's house, and the men of her city shall stone her with stones that she die: because she hath wrought folly in Israel, to play the whore in her father's house: so shalt thou put evil away from among you.

An Eastern wedding sometimes lasted for up to a year. Betrothal in their ceremony meant the couple was united in marriage. In other words, the betrothal aspect of the ceremony sanctioned a marriage union. However, the married couple came together for sexual intercourse upon a set date that would be sometime in the future. The bride remained in the home of her parents; who guarded her virginity. On the occasion of the married couple coming together, in sexual intercourse for the first time, they slept on a cloth designed to confirm the sexual faithfulness of the wife. Bloodstains from the ruptured hymen of the wife provided proof of her virginity. If the wife had engaged in sexual relations with a third party (someone other than her husband) she had then become an adulteress. The penalty for adultery under the law was death by stoning. God provided protection for a bride and her family by this law.

The wife could not just be hauled-off and put to death on the false grounds claimed by a deceitful husband. Even though the penalty for adultery was to be put to death by stoning, the heart of the law allowed mercy and forgiveness. Joseph's relationship with Mary is a good example of mercy being given to one thought to be an adulteress. Joseph had decided to put his wife away in a private manner rather than making a public example of her. We know that he changed his mind after having received the news that Mary was pregnant by means of the Holy Spirit.

The Law of Moses did not provide a provision that justified divorce; God did not sanction it by a statute. However, the law God gave to Moses did regulate the man-made practice of husbands divorcing their wives. God instituted a way to restrain the marital abuse that was being practiced upon married women; they could no longer be put away without some stated reason as to why. The bill of divorcement told why they were put away. At this point we need to look carefully at what is said in the following verses:

Deuteronomy 24:1-4:
When a man hath taken a wife, and married her, and it come to pass that she find no favour in his eyes, because he hath found some uncleanness in her: then let him write her a bill of divorcement, and give it in her hand, and send her out of his house. And when she is departed out of his house, she may go and be another man's wife. And if the latter husband hate her, and write her a bill of divorcement, and giveth it in her hand, and sendeth

her out of his house; or if the latter husband die, which took her to be his wife; Her former husband, which sent her away, may not take her again to be his wife, after that she is defiled; for that is abomination before the Lord: and thou shalt not cause the land to sin, which the Lord thy God giveth thee for an inheritance.

Some have misinterpreted the phrase "some uncleanness" to be a reference to sexual sin; that of fornication. Jay E. Adams' treatment of this phrase is superb.

> The Hebrew words are *erwath dabar.* They have been translated in any number of ways, including, "something indecent," "something shameful," "some indecency," etc. Literally, the two Hebrew words are "a matter of nakedness." They seem to mean something indecent, disgusting or repulsive. Almost all interpreters agree with John Murray when he says: (there is no evidence to show that *erwath dabar* refers to adultery or an act of sexual uncleanness . . . We may conclude that *erwath dabar* means some indecency or impropriety of behavior.) [25]

(John Murray was professor of Systematic Theology at Westminster Theological Seminary. His work *Divorce* gives a study of *erwath dabar.*) These same Hebrew words are used in reference to an unclean thing in Deuteronomy 23:12-14. There is no reference to sexual sin in this passage either. The emphasis of thought in Deuteronomy 24 is dealing with anything that a husband might think to be reason enough to put away his wife. The passage is not condoning his decision or his behavior; rather, it is declaring that no matter what the reason for putting her away, <u>he must</u> provide her a written bill of divorcement. The action of the divorced wife is also addressed. If she remarries and divorces again, or if her second husband dies, her original husband is not to remarry her. These are regulations about divorce; but they do not <u>sanction </u>the practice of divorce. Nor does this text offer any clarity concerning the reason the man may have decided to divorce his wife.

OLD TESTAMENT MARRIAGE

In Matthew 19, a group of Pharisees solicited the opinion of Jesus Christ about divorce. They were testing his words, trying to trap him. The question they put forth to him asked, "Is it lawful for a man to put away his wife for every cause?" We know from the Gospel record that these Pharisees were good at leaving the weightier matters of the law undone. This is what they were trying to do on this occasion. They were trying to justify their practice of putting away their wives; a practice not permitted by God in the beginning. The answer they received from Jesus was:

Matthew 19:4-6:
And he answered and said unto them, Have ye not read, that he which made them at the beginning made them male and female, and said, For this cause shall a man leave father and mother, and shall cleave to his wife: and they twain shall be one flesh? Wherefore they are no more twain, but one flesh.

What therefore God hath joined together let not man put asunder.

This is not what they wanted to hear. They were not interested in preserving a marriage for a lifetime. Instead, they wanted to preserve what they claimed was their right to divorce a wife, if they were inclined to do so. They wanted the ability to "put her asunder." It did not matter to them what God had said in the beginning. Their total disregard of what God said about marriage was so obvious. What they thought they understood from the law in Deuteronomy 24 formed the basis of their next question. They ask Jesus, "Why did Moses then command to give a writing of divorcement, and to put her away" (Matthew 19:7)?

Their frame of reference was Deuteronomy 24. They referred to Moses' "command to give a written bill of divorcement," as a proof that they were justified in putting away a wife by divorcing her. These Pharisees claimed that Moses "commanded" divorce; however, Moses did nothing of the kind. Jesus set their perspective straight and declared that Moses only permitted divorce; he did not condone the practice. (There may have been two rabbinical schools of thought about divorce at that time; one restricting the causes for divorce, and the other allowing a liberal, non-restrictive view—divorce for almost any reason. If there were two schools of thought, both were wrong.) The law did not give a single reason that would justify divorcing their wives.

Moses, in Deuteronomy 24, did not name a particular case study as a reference for what he was teaching. He was instead, making a general statement. His statement in essence was, "for whatever reason you put away a wife," you must give her a written bill of divorcement. No matter what the reason for the divorce, the bill of divorcement must be given her. The written bill of divorcement, called for by this law, terminated a marriage union and it gave the details of why the wife was put away. By this law, God instituted a way to restrain the hardhearted marital abuse that husbands were practicing against their wives. This was the purpose for the law. It was never a justification for a divorce. The Pharisees had misapplied the Scripture they were quoting as a basis for their position. Below is the response they received from Jesus:

Matthew 19:8-9:
He saith unto them, Moses because of the hardness of your hearts suffered you to put away your wives: but from the beginning it was not so. And I say unto you, Whosoever shall put away his wife, except it be for fornication, and shall marry another, committeth adultery: and whoso marrieth her which is put away doth commit adultery.

The answer Jesus offered was clear and it cut to the heart of the matter. These Pharisees did not get the justification they sought, because there was no justification for their practice of divorcing their wives. They hoped that Jesus would take an unpopular stance with what he taught concerning divorce. He did just that and it was far more unpopular than they could have imagined. Jesus could see that their hardheartedness towards their wives was their real problem. The real difficulty they were having was not with their wives, but it lay within the recesses of their own hardened hearts.

The "hardness of heart issue," which led men to put away their wives in the days of Moses, has never been eradicated. The Pharisees that stood before Jesus had a big dose of this same problem. This same issue continues to motivate married couples to divorce one another in our day also. Husbands and wives throughout history have sought to justify their inability to live in a loving relationship with their mate. Just like those hardhearted Pharisees, they have manufactured what they believe to be watertight justifications for putting a mate away. Most of these so-called justifications are nothing more than modern day "cop-outs." After these excuses are stripped away, the real problem is laid bare; it's still callousness of heart. It was hardness of heart in the days of Moses, and of Jesus Christ, and it's still hardness of heart today.

- It is hardness of heart when a husband or a wife can't muster up forgiveness.
- It is hardness of heart that can't love with the love of God.
- It is hardness of heart that won't look inside of one's own heart to see what might be out of order there.
- It is hardness of heart that insists, divorce is justified and, "there's just no other way."

Jesus directed the attention of those men to the marriage standard God established in the beginning. By the way, the standard God established from the beginning has never <u>changed</u>. It's one husband and one wife for life. To this very day, this is still God's will. This is the best there is! The need is that we get with God's program and leave-off with our man-made solutions for marriage difficulties. The pages in our Bible are loaded with the precise counsel that will heal every marriage difficulty. It's the putting away of one's mate, for a non-biblical reason and marrying another, that is the bigger problem; Jesus called doing so an adulterous act.

We may need some clarity about the difference between adultery and fornication. The general notion that fornication is sexual sin between the unmarried, and adultery is sexual sin that involves a married person, is not biblical. Biblically, adultery refers to a breach in the marriage covenant of faithfulness. The breach occurs when a third person is allowed to interfere, usually in a sexual manner, and disrupt the covenant of faithfulness between a husband and wife. So, adultery is the sin of unfaithfulness by a marriage partner. Fornication is sexual sin of any type. Homosexuality, incest, group sex, lesbianism, bestiality, sex between the unmarried, and adultery, are all sexual sins that come under the biblical description of fornication. Adultery is included in this list because it is a sexual sin. Fornication is the means by which the adultery occurs.

Sinfully divorcing a marriage partner, for a non-biblical reason, and marrying another is an ardent, adulterous act. Outside of an act of fornication, (sexual sin), and physically heinous acts, there is no biblical justification for divorce. (We will deal with the issue of physical abuse later.) This was what Jesus declared here in the above verse (Matthew 19:9). What Jesus was teaching in this passage is based squarely on Deuteronomy 24, with the exception of what he declared about fornication.

In our day it is a common practice to divorce a marriage partner for a frivolous, non-biblical reason, and shortly thereafter marry someone new. This action does not measure up to the high standard of God's Word. It is an adulterous, sinful, practice that remains contrary to what is taught by the Bible. The question becomes whose will is going to stand; will it be the will of God, or will it be the will of a man? There will always be a godly way to keep that marriage from falling apart. Jesus did not teach that a marriage partner "must" be put away because of fornication. The godly option of forgiveness is available and can be practiced by any individual with a forgiving heart. Forgiveness offered to a repentant mate will be the best solution for a marriage that is falling apart.

James 2:13:
For he shall have judgment without mercy, that hath shewed no mercy; and mercy rejoiceth against judgment.

THE EXCEPTION CLAUSE

The Law itself never justified the putting away of a wife because of fornication. Plainly stated, the Law never justified divorce for any reason. It was not upon the Old Testament law that Jesus based his statement about fornication being a justifiable reason to divorce a marriage partner. He based this statement upon the actions of his Heavenly Father—God's figurative marriage to the nation of Israel was the basis of his teaching. Many of the Old Testament prophets compare God's relationship with Israel to that of a husband and wife. It was from his understanding of God's figuratively marriage relationship with Israel that Jesus established the "exception of fornication" teaching. A short review of God's marriage relationship with Israel will help us to see what we need to understand.

Ezekiel 16:8-16:
Now when I passed by thee, and looked upon thee, behold, thy time was the time of love; and I spread my skirt over thee, and covered thy nakedness: yea, I sware unto thee, and entered into a covenant with thee, saith the Lord God, and thou becamest mine. Then washed I thee with water; yea, I throughly washed away thy blood from thee, and I anointed thee with oil. I clothed thee also with broidered work, and shod thee with badgers' skin, and I girded thee about with fine linen, and I covered thee with silk. I decked thee also with ornaments, and I put bracelets upon thy hands, and a chain on thy neck. And I put a jewel on thy forehead, and earrings in thine ears, and a beautiful crown upon thine head. Thus wast thou decked with gold and silver; and thy raiment was of fine linen, and silk, and broidered work; thou didst eat fine flour, and honey, and oil: and thou wast exceeding beautiful, and thou didst prosper into a kingdom. And thy renown went forth

among the heathen for thy beauty: for it was perfect through my comeliness, which I had put upon thee, saith the Lord God.
But thou didst trust in thine own beauty, and playedst the harlot because of thy renown, and pouredst out thy fornications on every one that passed by; his it was. And of thy garments thou didst take, and deckedst thy high places with divers colours, and playedst the harlot thereupon: the like things shall not come, neither shall it be so.

God covered Israel with his skirt in taking her for a bride; and, Oh, He treated her so well! He showered her with His goodness and love. However, God's loving goodness was not enough to please his wife, Israel. Even before entering the Promised Land she played the whore by forsaking her Husband and sought out other gods to worship. Her fornication and her unfaithfulness continued century after century. All along, her Husband, God, showed forth His loving kindness, and willingness to forgive her (Jeremiah 3:1). He exercised tremendous patience and longsuffering toward His wife. He called upon her to repent and live faithfully as she had promised to do; but she would not repent and change her ways. Finally, because she would not put away her fornication and unfaithfulness, God put her away.

Hosea 2:2:
Plead with your mother, plead: for she is not my wife, neither am I her husband: let her therefore put away her whoredoms out of her sight, and her adulteries from between her breasts.

Because of Israel's unrepentant heart, her Husband, God, put her away. He gave her a bill of divorcement. Yet still, God's plan is to marry her again. By God's grace and mercy, by His loving kindness, Israel is, one day, to be restored. Israel will become His bride again. This is still a future occurrence; but nonetheless, during the millennial reign of the Lord Jesus Christ, this is what God will do. The accomplished reality of restoration between God and Israel is a certainty.

This is the example Jesus based his "except it be for fornication" teaching upon. He understood that God's every effort was to find a remedy whereby the fornication of His wife could become a thing of the past. However, Israel would not respond by repentance, and finally this is why God (utilizing a man-made practice) divorced her. God utilized this wayward practice of men as a teaching tool and employed it here in His relationship with Israel—you put away your wives and now you will be put away! Even though He put her away, God's heart remains open to a wonderful day of reconciliation. The union He shares with Israel is a lasting union that will go on throughout eternity.

Jeremiah 31:35-37:
Thus saith the Lord, which giveth the sun for a light by day, and the ordinances of the moon and of the stars for a light by night, which divideth the sea when the waves thereof roar; The Lord of hosts is his name: If those ordinances depart from before me, saith the Lord, then the seed of Israel also shall cease from being a nation before me for ever. Thus saith

the Lord; If heaven above can be measured, and the foundations of the earth searched out beneath, I will also cast off all the seed of Israel for all that they have done, saith the Lord.

Obviously none of these things will ever occur. The point here is very clear, God will never cast off Israel; His divorce with her is only a temporary measure. The ups and downs, the failures and heartaches, that strained His marriage union, will not destroy it— no, not even Israel's fornication and adultery. This is how big God's gracious love for His bride (His people) is. He will not give up on them; "For the Lord, the God of Israel, saith that he hateth putting away" (Malachi 2:16). Jesus understood God's reluctance to put His wife away. He understood that God put her away as a means to bring His unrepentant wife to her senses that she might finally repent and turn again to her husband in faithfulness.

Jesus understood the entirety of God's marriage relationship with Israel, and we need to understand it also. God's figurative marriage with Israel is a dynamic picture of the matrimony we need to practice. It is the prototype of what marriage is and how it works. We know this is true because this is the example that God Himself has lived out before us. By following the clarity of His example we can begin to understand marriage at its best. The tearing apart by divorce is man-made. The fulfilling union of marriage is God made. God's personal example of marriage must become the steadfast standard for husbands and wives. In the ungodly event that some detrimental obstacle breaches a couple's union, their next efforts must be restoration. Charitable love, understanding, and gracious forgiveness— just like that of our Heavenly Father's, can foster restoration. Forgiveness, mercy, grace and thankfulness make up a big part of the fuel that is needed to keep a marriage alive and travelling ahead in the right direction.

After the big discussion about divorce with the Pharisees was over, (as recorded in Matthew 19:8-9) some of Jesus' disciples sought a little more insight about what was taught. Their conclusion gives us a glimpse into some of the harsh marriage relationships that existed among men and women in their day. These disciples, just like the Pharisees, wanted the latitude to put a wife away if they thought it was necessary to do so. In response to what Jesus had taught, they stated the following: "If the case (position) of the man be so with his wife, it is not good to marry" (Matthew 19:10). In other words, if this is the way it must be, it's better not to marry. They thought that the requirement of an enduring marriage, Jesus had just described, might be more than they could fulfill—or were willing to fulfill. Their thinking was, if we can't put her away for a reason that we think is justifiable, then it's better to stay unmarried. They were wrong about this. Jesus did not agree with their conclusion. As we saw earlier, certain categories of individuals have no need for marriage. However, most individuals have the need of companionship, and for this reason choose to marry. The disciples were at least right about one thing. The requirement of a lifetime marriage commitment is indeed a weighty decision. It is essential that individuals entering marriage embrace the unmitigated reality that their union should last until they die.

A COVENANT OF SALT

A tremendous eastern custom that couples can make a part of their marriage ceremony is the salt covenant. They will need to thoroughly understand the complete significance of it before they choose to observe it. This covenant is a pledge of fidelity; a promise unto the death. The Bishop K. C. Pillai's little book, *Light Through An Eastern Window*, has a chapter which explains some of the details and significance of the covenant of salt. Regarding the covenant being utilized in a marriage ceremony he writes:

> In the first chapter we mentioned that the bride and groom also take the salt covenant when they repeat their vows. This is the reason that there is little or no divorce among the high caste Hindus in my country. Whenever the husband is tempted to mistreat his wife; or the wife thinks to nag her husband, they remember their covenant of salt, and adjust themselves accordingly.[26]

Whenever an Easterner participates in a salt covenant you can be assured that they will remain loyal. In their thinking, the penalty for breaking the salt covenant pledge is too big of a price to pay. There are many references to the use of salt in the Word of God. Some of them refer directly to the practice of the eastern salt covenant.

II Chronicles 13:5:
Ought ye not to know that the Lord God of Israel gave the kingdom over Israel to David for ever, even to him and to his sons by a covenant of salt?

Another good reference to salt is the following:

Mark 9:49-50:
For every one shall be salted with fire, and every sacrifice shall be salted with salt, Salt is good: but if the salt have lost his saltness, wherewith will ye season it? Have salt in yourselves, and have peace one with another.

MARRIAGE IN THE CHURCH EPISTLES— BELIEVER TO BELIEVER

The marriage relationship, addressed by the Old Testament law, was one Believer united with another. The Epistle of I Corinthians is addressed to the church of the body administration to which Christians belong today. It includes marriage instructions for Believers. It also addresses the marriage relationship of Believers united with unbelievers. We will look at Believer married to Believer first.

I Corinthians 7:10-11:
And unto the married I command, yet not I, but the Lord, Let not the wife depart from her husband: But and if she depart, let her remain unmarried, or be reconciled to her husband: and let not the husband put away his wife.

The Apostle Paul does not address the "except it be for for-nication" statement Jesus gave in Matthew 19:9. Jesus was addressing his teaching to men and women who were not born-again of God's spirit. They were individuals guided by the standard of the Old Testament law. Paul's message is addressed to the Church-of-the-Body. (The grace adminis-tration to which we belong today.) His words are addressed to married men and women that are born-again of God's spirit; they have the ability that comes by having Christ within them. They have the ability to love with the love of God. They have been the blessed recipients of God's for-giveness. God's great grace and mercy has cleansed them of their sins by the shed blood of Jesus Christ. Surely, surely, they also have the capacity to overcome marital tragedies. Even the horrific sin of fornication can be forgiven after the pattern of their Heavenly Father's example of forgiveness.

What we are dealing with, at this point, is divorce that is <u>not justified</u> on biblical grounds. Paul knew what the law said in Deuteronomy 24. Doubtless, he also knew of the dis-cussion Jesus had with the Pharisees. The revelation Paul sets forth here to married Believers is that they are not to separate by divorcing. (What God has joined together let not man put asunder. This is God's design for marriage; it's not to be put asunder.) What the apostle Paul is stating here in verse 10 is in full accord with what God established in Genesis. The command put forth above in verse 10 is, "DO NOT DIVORCE!" This is the standard of the Word of God. It is imperative that we realize when a couple comes together in a marriage ceremony they are standing before

God's presence in what they vow to each other. The presiding minister announces to the bride and groom: "In the presence of God and these witnesses, I now pronounce you man and wife. You may kiss the bride!" The bride and groom are promising before God to live together for the rest of their days. God is joining them together not to be put asunder.

Divorce is a man-made solution, which, in the end, is not a solution, but rather an aggravation. It frustrates healing because it divides and separates. It "masks" what needs to be confronted and corrected. The snare of the devil has successfully projected the belief that divorce is an okay way to dissolve a marriage union. Distraught couples mistakenly believe that what is going to occur after the divorce will be an improvement for their lives. (The TV show "Happily Divorced" projects to the public that this is true.) But, when couples are contemplating splitting up their marriage union the bottom-line issue they must face is a spiritual one. They are immediately confronted with a question that concerns their integrity, both unto themselves, and before God. They must "own-up" to the commitment of what they have promised to do.

The promise was, "I will live with this man or with this woman for the rest of my days." No buts! No excuses! No changing of the mind! No false justifications! The effort to justify divorce with made-up excuses leads to broken fellowship with our loving God. Honesty and honor travel together, hand in hand, but lying and deceiving is sin. It's by the keeping of our word that we build strong moral character. By keeping our word we please God. Keeping our lifetime marriage commitment is the honest thing to do. Remember that God honors marriage commitments, but divorce is a man-made attempt at a solution.

Please notice that in I Corinthians 7:11 (above) the conjunction "But" is a very big, BUT. If either the wife or a husband fails to heed the admonition of "let <u>not</u> the wife depart," or "let <u>not</u> the husband put away," and then goes ahead and divorces their mate, then what? If God's will is rejected; if that which both the Lord Jesus and the Apostle Paul taught about divorce is ignored, then what comes next? It's clear that God knew some married couples would plough through the STOP sign of what His Word says about divorcing a mate.

It is certainly not a difficult problem to get a judgment of divorce from a state government today. Couples can sue for a divorce for a multiplicity of non-biblical reasons. "No fault divorce" is the law in most every state of the union; they'll obligingly grant one, hands down; almost no questions asked. However, what is acceptable in the eyes of the government is not the biggest consideration. What is acceptable in the eyes of God is the biggest consideration for a Christian Believer. To please God comes first!

It is sad to see any marriage end in divorce; however, to see a CHRISTIAN husband and wife end their union is more than sad, it's a tragedy. In the eyes of a community, divorce speaks loudly; it's a public declaration. It says to all that know about it, this Christian man and woman stopped loving each other; at least one of them did. We Christian Believers are not to thwart the Gospel of the Lord Jesus Christ by what we do in any category of our lives. Our calling is a high calling. We are ambassadors for Christ. We need to remember who we are, and stay in character. We are the best God's got here on the face of the earth.

II Corinthians 3:2-3:
Ye are our epistle written in our hearts, known and read of all men: Forasmuch as ye are manifestly declared to be the epistle of Christ ministered by us, written not with ink, but with the Spirit of the living God; not in tables of stone, but in fleshy tables of the heart.

Our actions certainly do speak louder than our words. Before a Christian couple came together in marriage, they were a brother and a sister in Christ. Obviously, their marriage union is a continuation of their brother and sister in Christ relationship. Actually, it's an exalted brother and sister relationship, wherein they have coveted to show forth the excellency of God's Word to each other. They have promised to bestow upon each other's lives, tender, loving, care and companionship.

In my marriage ceremony I promised the following:

"I, Charlie, take you, Carol, to be my wife, to have and to hold from this day forward, to honor, to cherish, to sustain and to love with all my heart in every

251

situation under every condition, according to God's Holy Word; and thereto I pledge to you myself."

But, in a divorce, a husband or a wife is declaring: "I don't love this brother, in Christ"— "I don't want this woman, even though she is my sister in Christ." —"I can't forgive this man." —"I can't forgive this woman." In so doing, marriage partners have taken their focus off of God's Word, and they have reneged on what they promised before God, and each other, they would do. Their actions speak volumes; and, everyone who knows them reads the epistle of their lives. Their Christian witness goes down the "tubes," so to speak. We, who know them, become confused and perplexed about their divorcing. Our hearts love both of them and we hurt for both of them. We continue to perceive them as a couple; it's hard for us to understand and accept their broken union.

At this point, we are still addressing marriage relationships between Christian Believers. In I Corinthians 7:11, the word is: "But and if she depart, let her remain unmarried, or be reconciled to her husband." When divorce proceedings are concluded a marriage has been repudiated. The divorce is legitimate, even though it may have been based upon non-biblical grounds. They are not still married in God's eyes; nonetheless, His view is that they have participated in a "sinful divorce." So, now that the former marriage is dissolved, what's next for the divorcees? The next course of action is not to go out and find some new person to marry. This is certainly not what needs to be done in

God's eyes; He has said, "Don't do it!" The stop sign reads: STOP, DO NOT MARRY A NEW MATE.

Couples that divorce for the wrong reasons are to remain unmarried. But, what if they're lonely? —What if they're in need of companionship? —What if they're "horny" and need sex? —What if they're having a hard time financially? What if, what if, what if? What if, the Word of God knows best about this situation, and it absolutely does! Divorced couples are to remain unmarried for a purpose. They must remain unmarried to be in a position to be reconciled to their former mate. God's great patience toward His adulteress wife, Israel, is a good example to follow. Even though He put her away, God is willing to wait for the right conditions and then, finally, He will remarry His divorced wife. To pursue a new mate is going in the wrong direction; it continues one's opposition to what God has said should be done. It is not a different mate that a non-biblically divorced husband or wife needs; they need healing and reconciliation with the mate to whom they were married.

The process whereby their marriage can be restored is sorrow and repentance, forgiveness and acceptance. The divorced couple needs to get it right with the Word of God, and then they can get it right with one another. They departed when God said, "Don't depart." Their broken fellowship with their Heavenly Father needs to be restored. Their decision to divorce was not godly; it ignored what God said they <u>were not to do</u>. The over-powering need they have is to get honest before God and honest before each other. Sorrow for themselves must turn to sorrow for having broken God's Word and having divorced their mate. They must sorrow for their failure to live up to what they promised to do for each other.

II Corinthians 7:10:
For godly sorrow worketh repentance to salvation (wholeness) not to be repented of, but the sorrow of the world worketh death.

They must lay aside their selfishness and hurt, and seek to be reconciled to their mate. It is time for them to put away their sin, their selfishness, and their shame. When they put away their bitterness and hurt, they can forgive each other. The best next move is to remarry their former mate. By doing so their marriage vows are restored. By having restored their fellowship with God, and with each other, they can now build their lives together. If they choose not to become reunited with their former marriage partner, then they should live unmarried for the rest of their days.

PHYSICAL VIOLENCE AND HEINOUS ACTS

This topic will be a rather lengthy departure from our present discussion; however, it needs to be said somewhere, and this is a good place. (We will get back on topic in a few pages.) It is always very sad to learn of physical violence in a marriage. Where life and limb are involved, actions must be taken quickly to remedy such a situation. Physical abuse cannot be allowed to continue. Incest and molestation in a family relationship are abuses that cannot be tolerated. It's certainly difficult to understand how this behavior could go on within a marriage of Christian Believers. However, the "unrenewed" Christian mind is no better off than the natural man's earth-bound way of thinking.

Matthew 15:19: (The Amplified Bible)
For out of the heart come evil thoughts (reasonings and disputings and designs) such as murder, adultery, sexual vice, theft, false witnessing, slander, and irreverent speech.[27]

I Corinthians 6:9-10:
Know ye not that the unrighteous shall not inherit the kingdom of God? Be not deceived: neither fornicators, nor idolaters, nor adulterers, nor effeminate, nor abusers of themselves with mankind, nor thieves, nor covetous, nor drunkards, nor revilers, nor extortioners, shall inherit the kingdom of God.

It's time to put this way of life, far behind us. Those who fail to do so are asking for trouble, especially in a marriage relationship. As Christian Believers, we must control our thinking; our calling and our task is to become transformed by the renewing of our minds (Romans 12:2). The need is that we make a clean break with our past. We cannot remain "conformed" to the superficial standards of this world. We must put off the works of darkness. We must cling tightly to the standard of God's Word. Failure to do so can keep us caught-up within the "five-senses mentality" that we were living in before we became born-again of God's spirit.

Physical violence, molestation, incest, and other heinous acts, quickly destroy marriages. God has provided a sure pathway of deliverance for those who are involved in horrific marriage disruptions such as these. The power and authority of the body of Christ, the church, needs to be utilized on these occasions. By doing so, many of these horrendous marriage impediments can be cleared-up and resolved. The following record tells us exactly how this is to be done.

Matthew 18:15-17:
Moreover if thy brother shall trespass against thee, go and tell him his fault between thee and him alone: if he shall hear thee, thou hast gained thy brother. But if he will not hear thee, then take with thee one or two more, that in the mouth of two or three witnesses every word may be established. And if he shall neglect to hear them, tell it unto the church: but if he neglect to hear the church, let him be unto thee as an heathen man and a publican.

When a brother or a sister responds positively to having been confronted by witnesses, a marriage union can often be restored. Praise God! On the other hand, when a harsh, destructive, mate responds negatively, and refuses to repent and change their hardhearted behavior, nothing more can be done for that individual. When they will not seek forgiveness, and they have no intention of changing their mind, they have shunned God's pathway to deliverance. Every avenue that might have brought deliverance has now been exhausted. The individual, who refuses the confrontation of a marriage partner, witnesses, friends, and finally the confrontation of the church, can justifiably be divorced. Divorce in this sad situation is certainly biblically justified. God did not call us to suffer abusive physical injury from the hand of a marriage partner. The offended mate might graciously allow some time to pass before considering another marriage. The prayer of a righteous marriage partner availeth much (James 5:16). Remember that God is a God of miracles.

We need to consider a few issues about the term "abuse." The word "abuse" has become an over-used, frivolous, crutch word. It is often used to demonize actions and behavior that may be rather normal. There are many things that may be described as "abusive" when someone is seeking to justify "dumping" a marriage partner. Mental abuse, emotional abuse, abusive language, and many other terms can be levied against a marriage partner when a mate is seeking to justify their own opinion or position. In other words, what she calls mental cruelty, he might describe as her unwillingness to obey. This flaky kind of excuse making has really gotten out of bounds. Difficulties in marriage are to be overcome and problems are to be resolved. Obstacles are going to be a part of every marriage union. Flimsy excuses just won't do. A married couple ought not to turn into cowards when they look into the face of the enemy. Maybe they need to toughen up a little. After all, they have promised the stability of a lifetime union.

Spiritual attacks against the stability of a marriage union are going to continue. Satan specializes in busting up marriages; he is the destroyer. It's not against flesh and blood that we are wrestling in this life. It is against the spiritual wickedness perpetrated by the prince of the power of the air. He will certainly seek to destroy the sanctity and grace of a marriage. Christian husbands and wives will need to be on guard, and actively stand against his methods. God wants us to know how to handle satanic, fiery, darts when they are hurled against us.

As shocking as it may be, God included the following account in the Bible for a purpose. From it we can learn how to handle depraved behavior that might raise its ugly head in a Christian marriage. When wretched behavior creeps into a marriage union, or any fellowship of Christian Believers, it must be confronted and resolved.

> *I Corinthians 5:1-2:*
> It is reported commonly that there is fornication among you, and such fornication as is not so much as named among the Gentiles, that one should have his father's wife. And ye are puffed up, and have not rather mourned, that he that hath done this deed might be taken away from among you.

This was, of course, a lewd, shameful, act on the part of this father's son. Even though what was happening became common knowledge, the church fellowship had stood idly by. After all, no one enjoys confrontation; so they closed their eyes to the seriousness of it. What the church needed to do, in the face of this uncommon fornication, was to take

Divorce in the Bible

the necessary action for everyone concerned. They needed to sorrow for this man and with loving concern, and forthrightness of purpose, address the issue. With the absences of confrontation, this man had no reason to change his behavior; he was getting by with what he was doing. Not only that, the sinfulness of this man's life was an impediment to the spiritual well being of their church fellowship. They needed to let this man know, in no uncertain terms, "We will not allow fornication in the midst of our church." Finally, they had the good judgment to take the action called for by the Word of the Lord. They told the man, you must leave our fellowship; go and get this situation corrected. We are not going to allow fornication to continue among us.

Isn't it amazing how doing the right thing produces the right results? After having been confronted, this fornicator had to come to terms with what he was doing. It was by withholding fellowship from this man that he came to understand the seriousness of his unwholesome behavior. We need to remember that this man was born-again of God's spirit. In this situation he needed the stability and spiritual backbone of brothers and sisters in Christ who were willing to stand up and say, "We love you, but we are not going to allow this wicked behavior here among us. You have succumbed to a snare of the devil." And yes, the appropriate action they took produced the appropriate results. This man became convicted of his sinfulness; he sorrowed for his wrong, and he sought forgiveness and reconciliation. This is just what was needed for all concerned. Now, after he repented, this man needed to be comforted and encourage

259

by the Believers in the fellowship. With their loving help, he could get on with his life and again become a blessing to his spiritual family.

> *II Corinthians 2:6-8: (The Amplified Bible)*
> For such a one this censure by the majority (which he has received is) sufficient (punishment). So (instead of further rebuke, now) you should rather turn and (graciously) forgive and comfort and encourage (him), to keep him from being overwhelmed by excessive sorrow and despair. I therefore beg you to reinstate him in your affections and assure him of your love for him.[28]

Obviously, we are not going to throw every sinner out of our Christian Fellowships; if we did so, all of us would be on the outside looking in. But, by the same token, when a brother or sister has been overtaken by a snare of the devil, our work is not to sit idly by. Our work is to lovingly care for our brothers and sisters who make up the body of Christ. We are not to stand idly by and allow them to be suppressed and defeated by the hand of the adversary. Instead, we lovingly care for them; we fight for them, we pray for them, we serve them, we confront them, and when they repent we forgive them. We rejoice in their victories because truly, they are our victories also.

It is sad to say, but from time to time, hard situations involving physical violence, lewd behavior, and fornication of all kinds, do occur even in the marriages of Christian Believers. The rules of engagement that God has provided the church is the best way to handle these occurrences. Here in the Epistles to the Corinthians, the outline of what to do, and how to do it, resolved their problem. The man who was having sexual intercourse with his father's wife repented of his wrong; he was forgiven, and restored to their fellowship. We too, can confidently rely upon God's Word in difficult situations such as this one. It worked well for the First Century Christian Church on this difficult occasion. When we have the task of addressing difficult behaviors, that occasionally erupt among the ranks of those born-again of God's spirit, the Word of God has shown us what we need to do, and how to do it. We just need to do what it says, and the victories will come.

BELIEVER TO UNBELIEVER

The marriage union of a Believer wed to an unbeliever is the next category we are going to consider. In this group, as we shall see, there is a case in which divorce is biblically justified.

I Corinthians 7:12-16:
But to the rest speak I, not the Lord: If any brother hath a wife that believeth not, and she be pleased to dwell with him, let him not put her away. And the woman which hath an husband that believeth not, and if he be pleased to dwell with her, let her not leave him. For the unbelieving husband is sanctified by the wife, and the unbelieving wife is sanctified by the husband: else were your children unclean; but now are they holy. But if the unbelieving depart, let

> him depart. A brother or a sister is not under bond-
> age in such cases: but God hath called us to peace.
> For what knowest thou, O wife, whether thou shalt
> save thy husband? or how knowest thou, O man,
> whether thou shalt save thy wife?

Jesus addressed the Old Testament Believer-to-Believer marriage relationship in Matthew 19. Here, the Apostle Paul is teaching by divine revelation. He is addressing the marriage status of Christian Believers wed to unbelievers. The command is that a Believing marriage partner is not to put their unbelieving spouse away. Their marriage is to continue. After all, they both coveted by a marriage oath, to live together as companions for the rest of their days. One partner becoming a Christian Believer later on does not negate what was promised to each other in their marriage vows. The Christian partner is obligated to bless their unbelieving mate with charitable, gracious, love and respect. Their marriage should go on for the rest of their days. Because one of them is now a Christian Believer their union can be lifted up to higher standards of fulfillment.

Living a radiant Christian life in the presence of an unbelieving mate could be the very thing to bring about a much-needed change. Because of the Believing mate's beautiful example, the unbelieving mate could have a change of heart and become born-again. This would be the best thing that could occur for the two of them. However, even if this never occurs, the unbelieving spouse still benefits with the union the two of them share. In such a marriage relationship the blessings of sanctification are extended to the unbelieving mate.

Sanctification for the Believer involves separation from the ways of the world, and honoring God by the way they live. Sanctification provides tremendous benefits to those who are born-again. Believers enjoy God's watchful care and abundant blessings upon their life. For the unbelieving partner, it's almost like having both a rich uncle, and a paid in full insurance policy that they did not know they had. Actually, it's even better than that! An example of this beneficial relationship can be understood from the unbelieving husband's perspective in the following record:

> *I Peter 3:1-2:*
> Likewise, ye wives, be in subjection to your own husbands; that, if any [Husbands] obey not the word, they also may without the word be won by the conversation [the godly behavior] of the wives; While they behold your chaste conversation [godly behavior] coupled with fear [respect].

A Christian wife, who practices a godly life in her daily living, becomes a dynamic witness to an unbelieving husband. He sees her meekness and obedience, both to himself, and also to her Heavenly Father. He sees uprightness, respect, reverence, and a quiet spirit in the way she lives. (Boy, does he ever have a lot going for himself.) If this unbelieving husband is ever going to turn to God in belief, the gracious life that his wife lives before him can be the very thing that leads him to do so. This kind of influence is one of the reasons the Believing partner is to remain with their unbelieving mate. The sunshine in the Believing partner's life brings light to the darkness and gloom of this present evil world. The radiant example of a Christian wife can be the deciding factor that helps a spouse turn to God.

In the case of an unbelieving partner's decision to break the marriage with a divorce, a different course of action is to be followed. In this event, the Believing partner is to step aside and agree upon the divorce. Even in this strained marriage relationship, it's still sad to see a divorce. Broken hearts, sorrow, and loneliness may lay ahead for all involved in the relationship, especially so for the children. However, nothing more can be done in this situation; nothing profitable will be gained by trying to continue this union. Those who are born-again are called to peace.

In departing, the unbelieving mate will have broken what they promised to do. After all, the standard of God's Word means little or nothing to them. To the hardhearted and unbelieving, "The things of the Spirit of God are foolishness." (I Corinthians 2:14) After the divorce, the Believing partner is dissolved of any and all responsibility associated with the former marriage union. He or she is no longer bound by any further obligations. Because there are no longer any remaining obligations to the first union, the Believer is free to marry again, if one so chooses. The children of this former marriage union remain covered by the sanctification of the Believing parent, no matter with whom they now live. There still remains one sure and abiding condition to any new marriage—it must be to a Believer, born-again of God's spirit. By this time, I'm almost certain, he or she will have no problem deciding to choose a Believer for a marriage partner.

REMARRIAGE

There are several Scriptural references regarding remarriage that we need to look at now. In the case of remarriage for widows the instruction is as follows:

I Corinthians 7:8-9:
I say therefore to the unmarried and widows, It is good for them if they abide even as I. But if they cannot contain, let them marry: for it is better to marry than to burn.

Notice that the widows have been placed in the same category as others who are not married. For some widows, the need for companionship and the need to satisfy their sex drive will be the determining factors leading to remarriage. It's the pressing need of the individual that is most important. If they can be content without a marriage partner that's best—it's less complicated; otherwise, if they decide for marriage they have done no wrong. Contentment to stay put with their present marital status will give them the latitude to serve the body of Christ more freely.

I Corinthians 7:39-40:
The wife is bound by the law as long as her husband liveth; but if her husband be dead, she is at liberty to be married to whom she will; only in the Lord. But

she is happier if she so abide, after my judgment: and I think also that I have the Spirit of God.

Christian Believers do not live under the Law Administration of the Old Testament. However, the "law of their marriage commitment" binds all married couples. The spiritual reality is that they are bundled-up by a lifetime oath of companionship; it's 'til death do us part. The death of either partner breaks the marriage union, and thereby frees the widowed partner of all obligations to that union. The above verses stress again two very important considerations. If there is no pressing need, the individual will be better off to live without a new marriage partner. If the decision is for remarriage the Believer should choose only a mate born-again of God's spirit. (The reference to widows in Romans 7:2-3 teaches the same thing; the surviving mate is free to remarry if they choose to do so.)

The next reference to widows remarrying concerns those who are actually not mature enough, age-wise, to serve in an ordained capacity in the Christian church.

I Timothy 5:14:
I will therefore that the younger women [widows] marry, bear children, guide the house, give none occasion to the adversary to speak reproachfully.

Ordination of the younger widows could cause some serious conflicts in their lives. Their sexual and companionship needs could be a distraction in fulfilling their work of ministering the gospel. Their effectiveness is the question.

This is one reason they are encouraged to remarry. If the younger widows cannot contain sexually, and have a pressing need for companionship, then remarriage will be the right thing for them. Remember the prophetess, Anna, who ministered to Joseph and Mary in the temple? She was a widow of about 80 years. She lived with her husband for only seven years. She was one of those individuals who had no pressing need for remarriage.

It is a fact of life that older widows have less trouble staying faithful to their commitment to minister in the church. The same principle is at work here that we looked at earlier. The effectiveness of an unmarried individual can be less encumbered in the performance of their calling. The unmarried can devote their full attention to the work of the ministry. Any sexual conflict the younger widows might have about service in their church will be stayed-off by remarriage. Remarriage is the best thing for them to do. If they do remain single, they are to care for themselves. The church is not to be charged with the care of younger widows. They must look to their Heavenly Father for His supply. Family members are also charged with the care of their own.

The next reference we will consider is a husband or a wife who has divorced their mate for the reason of fornication. Is remarriage a possibility for them? All who have divorced according to the biblical standard are free to remarry. However, please remember, Jesus addressed his words about divorcing, for the reason of fornication (Matthew 19:8-9), to those who were living under the law administration.

Married couples, born-again of God's spirit, should live by a higher law—the law of love. When a mate has been put away, remarriage to that former mate is certainly desirable. This is what God will do for his bride Israel. Remember that there is not a biblical command that a marriage partner <u>must</u> be put away. Hard hearts can soften and heal; attitudes can change. Repentance and forgiveness are the avenues that must be traveled for this to take place. But, if there is no reconciliation with the divorced partner and the decision is for marriage to a new partner, then what? Because the divorce terminated the marriage, and there are no further obligations to fulfill, the "injured" partner is no longer bound by the union, and is therefore free to remarry. The same two important considerations we saw above in I Corinthians 7:39-40 are applicable here also. If there is no pressing need, it's best not to remarry. If the decision is for remarriage choose only a mate born-again of God's spirit.

Is it biblically right for one who has been divorced for fornication to remarry? This definitely needs to be answered. But, before doing so, we need to consider a few side issues. The current loose standard of our society, which shrugs off the seriousness of adultery, is not a standard to rely upon; it's a deceptive, lying, standard. This loose standard is a "suck-hole" that draws people into the delusional thinking of, "What's the big deal?" However, the true trustworthy standard involves spiritual understanding. The absolute authority of God's Word, and what it declares about fornication and adultery, must surely become the standard of every born-again Believer. What was it that led to this sinful behavior; and, why did this husband or wife get involved with someone else in the first place?

A marriage partner, who has sinned by the act of fornication, has fallen into a snare of Satan's making. By maintaining an unwholesome relationship, they have gotten into more trouble than they thought about. Their inflated ego, their lust, and their selfishness have gotten them into really "hot water." They did not flee temptation, but yielded to it. They have sinned against God. The covenant of faithfulness, they swore to uphold, they have broken. Now, they have been put away by the mate whom they have forsaken and seriously wronged.

The serious consequences of fornication and adultery must be understood. There are two examples that can help us see God's perspective in situations where adultery was involved. The first one is the occasion of Pharaoh, King of Egypt, taking Abraham's wife Sarah into his court for the purpose of making her his wife. The results of this action was, God plagued Pharaoh's house with great plagues because he had taken Sarah from Abraham (Genesis 12). The second record is the occasion of Abimelech, a Philistine king, taking Abraham's wife Sarah into his court to make her his wife. The message Abimelech received from God about this matter was that if he failed to restore Sarah to Abraham, "Both you and all that are yours will surely die" (Genesis 20). From the high peek of Mt. Sinai, God spoke in an awesome, audible, voice to the Children of Israel. His proclamation to them was, "Thou shalt not commit adultery" (Exodus 20:14). By a statue of Old Testament law, the punishment for adultery was death. No bigger penalty could be paid than the loss of an individual's life. The book of Proverbs accentuates the seriousness of adultery in the following record. Here we find some vivid clarity about the consequences of adulterous behavior. In the following account a husband is away on a business trip. While he is away his wife lured a young man into her bed for sex.

Proverbs 7:13-27:
So she caught him, and kissed him, and with an impudent face said unto him, I have peace offerings with me; this day have I payed my vows. Therefore came I forth to meet thee, diligently to seek thy face, and I have found thee. I have decked my bed with coverings of tapestry, with carved works, with fine linen of Egypt. I have perfumed my bed with myrrh, aloes, and cinnamon. Come, let us take our fill of love until the morning: let us solace ourselves with loves. For the goodman is not at home, he is gone a long journey: He hath taken a bag of money with him, and will come home at the day appointed. With her much fair speech she caused him to yield, with the flattering of her lips she forced him. He goeth after her straightway, as an ox goeth to the slaughter, or as a fool to the correction of the stocks; Till a dart strike through his liver; as a bird hasteth to the snare, and knoweth not that it is for his life. Hearken unto me now therefore, O ye children, and attend to the words of my mouth. Let not thine heart decline to her ways, go not astray in her paths. For she hath cast down many wounded: yea, many

strong men have been slain by her. Her house is the way to hell, going down to the chambers of death.

The Old Testament Scriptures were written for our learning; that we might be comforted and encouraged by what they teach us. The Church Epistles are addressed directly to all that are born-again of God's spirit. They teach us to avoid fornication—it's for our own good to do so.

I Corinthians 6:18:
Flee fornication. Every sin that a man doeth is without the body; but he that committeth fornication sinneth against his own body.

Fornication is the pathway of self-destruction; it's a burning fire that sears every hand that touches it. Its fleeting pleasure is marred by the exacting penalty brought upon those who choose it. The bright lights, which promote enticing loose sexual intercourse, never get around to explaining the exacting penalty that will be paid for participating. A good example of the price to be paid for adultery is David's shameful sexual relationship with Uriah's wife, Bathsheba. King David's adulterous behavior with her brought about grievous results—first to himself, but also to those around him. Bathsheba's pregnancy could not be hid, so David decided to have her husband murdered. By the way, Uriah was one of his most loyal, trusted, servants. David committed this act in a sly, secretive way to make it look like he had nothing to do with it. He then took Uriah's wife and made her his wife. David's secret was not a secret to God. God sent Nathan the prophet to give the following message to David.

II Samuel 12:10-14:
Now therefore the sword shall never depart from thine house; because thou hast despised me, and hast taken the wife of Uriah the Hittite to be thy wife. Thus saith the Lord, Behold, I will raise up evil against thee out of thine own house, and I will take thy wives before thine eyes, and give them unto thy neighbour, and he shall lie with thy wives in the sight of this sun. For thou didst it secretly: but I will do this thing before all Israel, and before the sun. And David said unto Nathan, I have sinned against the Lord. And Nathan said unto David, The Lord also hath put away thy sin; thou shalt not die. Howbeit, because by this deed thou hast given great occasion to the enemies of the Lord to blaspheme, the child also that is born unto thee shall surely die.

David paid an exacting price for his adulterous behavior, and so does everyone who gets involved in an adulterous affair. Everything Nathan prophesied about David's life came to pass. The great example David shows us here in this record is that he got off the road of destruction he was traveling. He repented before God for his sinful behavior, and God put away his sin.

We have clearly seen that the command of God's Word is to steer-clear of fornication, and the consequences it is certain to bring. Christian husbands and wives are to avoid fornication, like the plague. They are to keep their egos in check. They are to honor God by living up to what they promised before Him they would do. They are to remove themselves from environments that are filled with sexual enticements and temptations. They are to remain faithful to their spouse. No extra-marital sex <u>period</u>—today or any other day, and that's the end of it!

Now we can get back to answering the question we asked earlier; is it biblically right for one who has been divorced for fornication to remarry? After having been divorced for the sexual sin of fornication, there are two roads the divorced partner can travel. They can continue traveling upon the road to destruction they are already on. Broken fellowship with their Heavenly Father is the detour that put them upon this roadway. Remarriage to a new partner is out of the equation for them. There are far too many issues that need to be resolved before any remarriage consideration. If they remain hardhearted and unrepentant about their sin, there is little that can be done on their behalf. They should not remarry! The better road to travel, for one divorced for fornication, is to turn to their loving Heavenly Father and repent of the wrong they have done. Restored fellowship with God is a must. Sorrow and repentance about their sins are the required elements that will restore their fellowship with Him. Restored fellowship will bring deliverance for them. God forgives the sin of fornication / adultery. David turned to God in repentance and received forgiveness for adultery and murder. The next thing the individual must do is to face up to the hurt, sorrow, and wrong they brought to their former mate. They should seek the forgiveness of the mate they have wronged. Remarriage to their former partner may be a possibility. This would be the best for all concerned. If that is not an option, then they could consider marriage with a new mate, but only to one born-again of God's spirit.

There are so many twists and turns related to this subject that it's a little difficult to cover all of them. Here is a category that we have not yet addressed. Those who have divorced their mates in a sinful fashion (not biblically justified) are not free to remarry without first addressing their failure. An example of this would be the Christian mate who has sinfully put away a non-believing mate. They must first repent and seek forgiveness. I am sure there are other categories that might be discussed. There is just not enough space to address them here. However, no matter what the situation may involve, the standard of God's Word is the rule by which it is to be measured.

SOME SUMMARY REMARKS

A few words of conclusion are in order here. We have seen some of the complications that surround divorce. We have discovered that divorce is a human invention and that it contradicts what God intended. Men and women have relied upon it for a scapegoat, to "weasel-out" of what they promised to a marriage partner. We have seen that the Old Testament law regulated divorce, but it never justified it. Jesus taught individuals who lived under the law administration that fornication (sexual sin) was a justification for divorce; however, nowhere in God's Word is divorce required for the reason of fornication. The decision as to what to do in such a situation is left up to the individual husband or wife. A sorrowing and repentant mate can and should be forgiven. The one instance where divorce is required is the occasion of an unbelieving marriage partner's decision to leave his or her union with a Believing partner.

We have seen that Jesus based his teaching about divorce for fornication upon the figurative marriage union that God shared with Israel. Even though God put Israel away, we have seen that because of His loving forgiveness He will remarry Israel again one day. Forgiveness and reconciliation have always been better solutions for marriage difficulties than seeking a divorce. God Himself has shown us how to behave in a marriage union. He has shown us, by example, how to be a husband and how to behave towards an erring wife. We can see His loving examples of patience, mercy, and forgiveness. We can see His forbearance and longsuffering, and we can see His wondrous grace in action. All this He bestowed upon his wife (Israel) despite her fornication and adultery and all her other shortcomings. He is going to take her back!

God is the example we must follow in our decisions about marriage and divorce. In doing so we will get it right! The need is that we behave like our Heavenly Father; this after all, is our high calling. We are asked to be imitators of God because we are His children.

Matthew 5:44-48:
But I say unto you, Love your enemies, bless them that curse you, do good to them that hate you, and pray for them which despitefully use you, and

persecute you; That ye may be the children of your Father which is in heaven: for he maketh his sun to rise on the evil and on the good, and sendeth rain on the just and on the unjust. For if ye love them which love you, what reward have ye? do not even the publicans the same? And if ye salute your brethren only, what do ye more than others? do not even the publicans so? Be ye therefore perfect, [spiritually mature, a spiritual giant] even as your Father which is in heaven is perfect.

In the gospel of John, Jesus prayed that we might be one with him and with our Heavenly Father (John 17:21). The first priority we have in life is to be one with God, to maintain fellowship with Him. When this is true of us, (that we are one with Him, walking with Him in peace and understanding) we are then prepared to bring outstanding qualities to a marriage relationship. We are prepared to manifest patience, loving kindness, mercy and forgiveness, to our wonderful mate. This is because we have chosen to behave just like our Heavenly Father. Godly characteristics like these are the true building blocks of a successful marriage; they are the qualities that enrich and build-up a marriage union. They will build a sturdy marriage structure that will not crumble in divorce.

CHAPTER 7

THE REVITALIZATION
OF CHRISTIAN
MARRIAGE

⁓

Today, the devastating influence of Christians divorcing each other for non-biblical reasons is undermining the testimony of God's Word. The example of Christian husbands and wives bound together by inseparable love and fidelity has become a rarity in our culture. What people are seeing in the Christian Community today is the ugly work of divorce rearing its head and becoming a common practice. Christian homes and families are torn apart by the same godless behavior that is common among God-rejecters. The shining example of Christian marriage is tarnished and growing dimmer and dimmer.

Confidence in what the Bible teaches about marriage needs to be restored. The disastrous appearance of failed Christian marriages needs to become a thing of the past.

The higher standard of marriage according to God's Book (our Bibles) must be embraced for this to occur. The outstanding need for every Christian husband and wife is that their marriage flowers and blooms into the beautiful, dynamic, relationship God intended. The fulfillment of a gratifying marriage union is certainly available. The following are some of the actions that <u>must</u> come to pass in order to revitalize the reputation of Christian marriage. These things <u>must</u> occur before the image of Christian marriage can be healed of its hypocrisy. Only then will Christian marriage become the witness God intended it to be.

WHAT THE CHURCH NEEDS TO DO

The Christian Community as a whole must embrace the standard of biblical marriage. Pastors and church leaders must embrace the truth and accuracy of God's Word and rely upon its standards and its precepts—especially so in this category of marriage. They need to teach their people to love and respect God's Word and what it teaches about marriage. Presently, they are allowing the unwholesome marriage standards of our flaky, weird society to go uncontrolled. They will need to teach their people that God has "the last word" in matrimonial matters. Pastors and church leaders must insist that worldly marriage practices are detrimental to the well being of husbands and wives.

Why is the Christian Community so timid these days? There was a day when the local church would not allow open wickedness in its membership. Today who gets confronted? One might begin to wonder if some of these congregations would toss Lucifer out. It is high time that Christian brethren put timidity to one side. The Lord Jesus Christ was never timid. He did not hesitate to confront the Scribes and Pharisees, even his apostles. Addressing Peter's error of "worldly thinking" he said, "Get the behind me Satan." Church leadership and their congregations must expect God's people to live by the standard of their calling. The confrontation of evil is a must—resist the devil and he will flee. The badge of Christian sanctification needs to glow in this dark world. (We are <u>in</u> this world but we are not <u>of</u> this world.) Basically, husbands and wives make up the leadership of local Christian churches. They need to let the "light of their marriages" so shine before men that people everywhere will see the beauty and power of their lives and glorify their Father which is in heaven (See Matthew 5:14-16).

WHAT CHRISTAIN HUSBANDS NEED TO DO

Christian husbands must assume the major responsibility for the predicament their marriage is in. Their failure to provide "God authorized leadership" for their wives has become a major downfall. Their neglect of God's Word, slothfulness, timidity, fear and selfishness, has robbed them of their authority. They must be first to take the necessary actions to correct these shortcomings and failures and regain their rightful authority to lovingly rule their families.

- Christian husbands must come to the place that they are willing to honor their marriage covenant with a wholesome commitment to follow through with what they have promised.

279

- They can no longer abdicate their duty to provide leadership. They must fully assume the responsibility for their wife's care and well being.
- They are to love their wives after the pattern of the loving care Christ has for his Church.
- Husbands must exemplify the qualities that are to be honored in their homes: dignity, kindness, respect, courtesy, loyalty, honesty, thoughtfulness and so forth.
- They are to labor to provide a home, food, and clothing to keep their families safe and secure.
- They will not take their wife away from her primary duty to care for the home and mother their children. They will encourage their wife and praise the importance of her accomplishments in caring for their home.
- They will keep their wife free form "spot and wrinkles"—unencumbered with excessive duties that they themselves must shoulder.
- They will meet the sexual needs of their wife by maintaining a loving, giving, sexual relationship with her.
- They will never place the spiritual, physical, and financial well being of their families upon any other shoulders (wife, parents, children, church, or government.) [29]

A husband is totally responsible for his wife and family—they are his. To be successful as a husband he must exercise the wisdom to rely upon God. He will need to seek the provisions and blessing of his Heavenly Father day by day.

WHAT CHRISTAIN WIVES NEED TO DO

The dilemma faced by Christian wives today concerns a choice of loyalties. They must choose between living their lives based upon the precepts of modern-day feminist doctrines or loyalty to the biblical precepts of marriage. Loyalty to the biblical precepts of marriage is, by far, the right choice. However, this choice of loyalties must be made in the midst of a feminist stronghold. Feminist influence dominates American culture.

When Christian wives choose to live by the biblical precepts of marriage, they have joined a unique group of women. They have joined a minority group of Christian wives who are now completely out-of-step with the worldly modern-day image of marriage. Their bravery, their fearless hearts, their determination to do it God's way, is absolutely what a "sin sick" misguided culture needs to see. Those who have chosen to honor God and His Word have become lights in a world of darkness. They have put aside the anemic lifestyles that are predicated upon worldly values. They are done with a lifestyle of hypocrisy. They have chosen biblical marriage. These are the brave-hearted wives who are helping to revitalize the image of Christian marriage.

If the image of Christian marriage is to be revitalized in our day and time, a vast majority of Christian wives must practice biblical marriage. The fulfillment of their gratifying marriages is what the people around them need to see. Nothing short of this will get the job done. Consequently, the revitalization of Christian marriage will require an about-face from what is presently acceptable.

- Christian wives will need to put to one side the supposed gratification of being independent. This is true because marriage not only implies dependency—it demands it. (What he has is just what she needs, and want she has is just what he needs.) The feminist doctrine of independence in marriage is ungodly. Marriage is the godly means by which each other's needs are to be fulfilled. Husbands are to seek to fulfill the needs of their wives and wives are to seek to fulfill the needs of their husbands.

- The expectations Christian wives have of their husbands needs to be biblically based. The worldly-minded standards of great renown, great wealth, and lavish comforts are not biblical—they are fading temporal assets.

I John 2:15-16:
Love not the world, neither the things that are in the world. If any man love the world, the love of the Father is not in him. For all that is in the world, the lust of the flesh, and the lust of the eyes, and the pride of life, is not of the Father, but is of the world.

Wives should be thankful for what the work of their husband's hands provide.

Husbands do not need to be pressured into supplying the "fading trinkets" of this world. Husbands need to be supported in their quest to live a life of godly simplicity.

What lifestyle could be more dynamic? When a husband is putting forth his best effort to provide, he will certainly be pleased to have his wife's encouragement and support.

- Christian wives need to show forth the modesty the Word of God asks of them. A meek and a quiet spirit are of great worth in the eyes of God. These tremendous qualities are also a prize to the life of any husband. The rough, tough, haughty spirit of a wife brings confusion and dismay into the atmosphere of marriage. When people gaze upon this kind of behavior they observe a wife in rebellion. She is rebelling against what the Word of God asks of her. The contradictions in her life will be fully evident.
- Wives need to provide warm, responsive, gratifying sexual intercourse for their husband. Just like the lyrics of a once popular song suggest—no other woman should be woman enough to take your man. The biblical duty is that husbands and wives are to meet the sexual needs of their mates. (And what a pleasurable duty it is meant to be.)
- Wives need to submit themselves to their husband. Husbands cannot force their wives to submit to them. Those who have tried to do so have found it a futile effort. Biblically, the wife is responsible to make herself submissive. Submission in marriage is a matter determined by choices in the heart, not in the head. It cannot be based upon the way she is treated by her husband—of course it's helpful when he is a loving man. A Christian wife's choice to be submissive to her husband must be based upon what

God asks her to do. It is the pleasing of her Heavenly Father that must remain the joy in her heart. It is for this reason she can submit to her husband. She can do so confidently and joyfully because she loves and trust her Heavenly Father. She knows that God knows best!

- The Christian wife who has chosen to take a stand upon what God expects her to do in marriage is a radiant witness of truth. The beauty of the relationship she shares with her husband will prove the truthful reality that God knows best. Contention and controversy have been laid to rest. There are no contradictions between the way she chooses to live her life and what God asks her to do in her marriage. The hypocrisy is gone. What a strong testimony her life has become. She has become a faithful witness of the Lord Jesus Christ. She is a living testimony to the truth of God's Word. Her marriage has become a beacon of light that will draw men and women to God.

CONCLUSION

The biggest single hindrance to having a successful marriage centers on a failure to practically apply what God has taught us to do. When a husband and his wife rely upon the integrity of God's Word, and they put what it teaches into practice, they can expect to have a beautiful, gratifying marriage. They will not be disappointed in their expectations. On the other hand, failure by a husband and wife to practice the biblical standards laid before them, can lead to the breakdown of their union. They will not enjoy their expectations because their behavior will be out of harmony with what is required to have success. If they are not willing to do what the Word of God teaches them to do, their expectations will "fall to the ground." The right choice for all married couples is to embrace and practice, *Marriage According to His Book.*

Psalm 37:4-5:
Delight thyself also in the Lord: and he shall give thee the desires of thine heart. Commit thy way unto the Lord; trust also in him; and he shall bring it to pass.

END NOTES

[1] Stephanie Coontz, *Marriage, a History*, Penguin Books London, England, 2005. The book deals with the differences of marriage customs.

[2] Pew Research The Decline of Marriage and The Rise of New Families-released: Nov. 18, 2010 www.pewsovialtrends.org

[3] *The Amplified Bible*, Zondervan Corp., USA, Ebt Frances Siewert, 1987, p. 1740.

[4] Henry Zelley, Pub. 1899

[5] Jay E. Adams, *Marriage, Divorce, And Remarriage In The Bible*, Zondervan, Grand Rapids, Michigan, 1980, p.17.

[6] Debi Pearl, *Created To Be His Help Meet*, Michael and Debi Pearl NGJ Ministries, Pleasantville, TN. 2005, p.230.

[7] *The Amplified Bible*, p.1734.

[8] Bishop K. C. Pillai, *Light Through An Eastern Window*, Robert Speller and Son, New York, 1963, p.18

[9] *The Amplified Bible*, p.934.

[10] Dan B. Allender, Tremper Longman, *Intimate Allies*, Tyndal House Pub., Wheaton, Illinois, 1995, p.158

[11] Gary Thomas, *Sacred Marriage*, Zondervan, Grand Rapids, Michigan, 2000, p.69.

[12] George M. Lamsa, *Old Testament Light*, A. J. Holman Co. Philadelphia, 1978, p.552

[14] F. Carolyn Graglli, *Domestic Tranquility*, Spence Publisnhing Co., Dallas, 1998, p. 60.

[15] Mary Kassian, *The Feminist Mystique Mistake*, Crossway Books, Wheaton, Ill., 2005, p. 261.

[16] ibid., p. 69

[17] ibid., p. 209

[18] ibid., p. 200

[19] Pearl, *Created To Be His Help Meet*, p. 43.

[20] You can hear this song, at www.nosuchthingasluck.com

[21] Lamsa, *Old Testament Light*, p.587.

[22] James Strongs, *The Exhaustive Concordance of The Bible*, Hendrickson Publishers, Peadoby, MA. (submit) p. 984

[23] Pearl, *Created To Be His Help Meet*, p.236.

[24] *The Amplified Bible*, p.1838.

[25] Adams, *Marriage, Divorce, And Remarriage In The Bible*, p.63.

[26] Pillai, *Light Through An Eastern Window*, p.38.

[27] *The Amplified Bible*, p.1419.

[28] *The Amplified Bible*, p.1747

[29] Douglas Wilson, *Reforming Marriage*, Canon Press, Moscow, Idaho, 1995 p.141. Mr. Wilson has a list of needs addressed to men.

Scripture Index

7:11	250
7:12-16	261
7:17a	19
7:20	19
7:25	20
7:26-27	24
7:29-31	24
7:32-33	20
7:34b	159
7:39-40	265
11:3	80
11:4	88
11:5	89
11:7	96
11:8, 9, 11	84
13:4-7	95
14:34-36	189
15:33	40

II CORINTHIANS

2:6-8	259
2:14	42
3:2-3	251
5:14-15	82
5:19-20	17
6:14-18	40
7:10	253
9:6-7	161

EPHESIANS

3:14-21	224
4:11-13	169
4:31-32	114
5:21-22	167, 217
5:22	173
5:23-24	173, 217
5:25	174
5:25-27	92
5:28-29	71, 91
5:33	221, 222

PHILIPPIANS

2:3-5	161
2:15	120
4:8-9	11
4:8b-11	161

COLOSSIANS

3:17-18	175, 217
3:19	113

I THESSALONIANS

4:3-8	31

I TIMOTHY

2:9-12	188
2:9-15	218